The Best Primitive Survival Skills for Texas

Wes Adams PhD

DEDICATION

This book is dedicated to the family that allowed me to explore our land at
an early age and develop a deep appreciation for nature.

CONTENTS

ACKNOWLEDGMENTS

This book was designed to document and expand on existing knowledge of primitive survival skills. It is a guide for those who practice outdoor skills. The book provides all the content needed to be proficient at primitive survival and can be used as a field guide. The book relies heavily on other experts to back up the author's knowledge of edible plants and other survival-related skills. The book references many current experts to add credibility to the knowledge contained within this book's pages.

HOW TO USE THIS BOOK

This book is designed to incorporate technology to enhance learning and provide access to videos and other educational resources. QR codes provide access to video content, but the reader will need a QR code scanner downloaded on their mobile device. A person can access all linked information by downloading a free QR code-reading app. All current Smart Phones can use scanning applications. Should the Internet fail, all the information is contained in the printed material. The video playlists are supplemental, and all vital information is contained in the printed pages. The playlists allow new videos to be added without purchasing a new edition of the book. Playlists will be updated over time to provide more comprehensive survival skills training then single videos can alone.

The COVID 19 pandemic and the snowstorm of February 2021 in Texas demonstrated the importance of understanding necessary survival skills. Many people were caught unprepared when the power and water system failed and were forced to rely on the existing food delivery system to get vital supplies. If another pandemic arises and the food and water systems fail, the need to know survival skills and edible plants will be invaluable. The knowledge contained in this book will help individuals have a basic knowledge of primitive survival.

Debris Shelter
Type: Primitive Shelter

The book is not a comprehensive list of all types of primitive shelters. When building shelters for the first time, it is best to build small scale structures first. This process allows the person building the shelter to have a good plan and reduces the chance of wasting effort. There are many types of shelter designs (e.g., Wigwam, Wickiup, etc.). When long-term options are needed, the following shelters are easy to build and provide various protection from the environment. A brush-debris shelter is one of the simplest forms of survival shelter. The most common type of brush shelter has a central ridgepole at its center and is covered with limbs to form a skeletal frame covered with two to three feet of brush. The inside has only enough room for one or two people to fit inside. There is very little room between the shelter and the person inside. Making the shelter's living area helps to hold in metabolic heat, so it is not lost to the environment. This type of shelter is nothing more than a debris sleeping bag.

Strengths: Easy to build, easy to maintain, no tools required to build and very good insulation.
Weakness: Limited room, no fire inside, require insulation materials.
Materials: Requires a ridgepole, limbs, leaves or brush.

 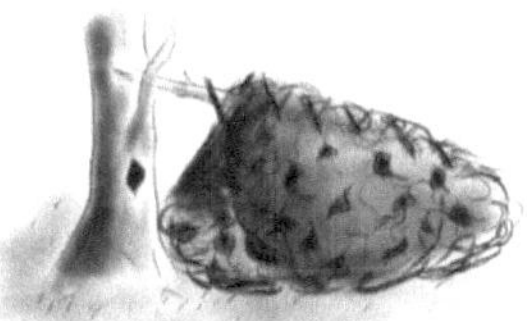

Figure 1. Debris Shelter. This figure illustrates a type of primitive debris shelter.

Lean-To Shelter
Primitive Shelter

A primitive lean-to is easy to build and requires no cordage. All that is needed is a strong ridgepole that can handle the weight of the brush. One of the best methods is to suspend the ridge pole between two sturdy trees, saving time and effort. A forty-five-degree angle is best to prevent the roof from leaking. The angle also provides sufficient protection from the elements. If the angle is too great, the structure will not provide adequate protection from the rain. If the angle is too low, the rain's surface tension will not pull the water down the structure, and the roof will leak. The brush's type and thickness are crucial elements to consider to prevent the roof from leaking and provide protection from the wind. A fire needs to be an adequate distance away to prevent the shelter from catching fire. If the brush is dry, it may accidentally combust. A fire reflector can be built to reflect heat into the structure.

Strengths: The shelter is easy to build, easy to maintain, no cordage or tools required to build.
Weakness: The roof can leak depending on materials and angle. The shelter is best for warm weather. The winds may shift, leaving a person vulnerable to the elements due to only one wall.
Materials: A Ridgepole, long limbs, brush, small trees with sufficient distance apart.

 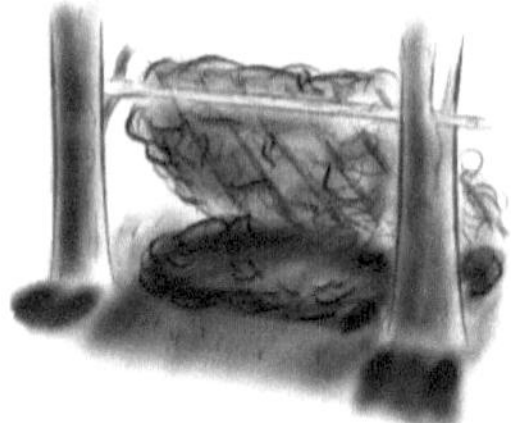

Figure 2. Primitive Lean-To Shelter. This figure illustrates a primitive lean-to shelter.

A-Frame Shelter
Primitive Shelter

A-frame shelter can be built by adding on to an existing lean-to shelter. A-frames have various forms that can be adopted based on the environment. A-frames are more open in warm, tropical locations. In colder environments, they can be well insulated with a dry brush. In tropical environments, many A-frames are modified with platforms to get the person off the ground. The platform can be used to elevate a person off the ground (e.g., jungle or/ swamps) to avoid insects and dangerous animals. It can also be used as an attic and filled in with some brush. The addition of brush allows for waterproofing, and almost any type of brush material can be used. In cold environments, the bottom floor can be walled in by weaving in saplings between the supports. The dead space between the walls can then be stuffed with leaves for additional insulation.

Strengths: A-frames can be built from a Lean-To. Primitive A-frames do not require cordage. In warm environments, a fire can be made inside depending on the type of A-frame built. It can be modified for warm and cold environments.
Weakness: The Roof can leak depending on materials used, more time-intensive.
Materials: A ridgepole, long limbs, leaves and brush.

Figure 3. Primitive A-frame Shelter. This figure illustrates a primitive A-frame shelter.

Ready-Made Shelter
Primitive Shelter

Ready-made shelters can save time and energy. In a survival situation, it is best to explore ready-made shelters to reduce caloric expenditure. Various natural resources function as shelters (e.g., caves, overhangs, fallen trees). Some are complete, requiring little work to act as sufficient shelter from the environment. Some need additional work to make them suitable to provide adequate shelter. All of the previously mentioned shelters building techniques can be used to enhance ready-made locations.

Strengths: Ready-made shelters require limited to no energy expenditure to create. Some are waterproof and provided excellent protection from the elements.
Weakness: Animals may already be using the shelter. Ready-made shelters may take time to locate.
Materials: Ready-made shelters may require limited to no resources to create adequate shelters.

Figure 4. Ready-Made Shelter. This figure illustrates fallen trees as a ready-made shelter.

Bow Drill
Primitive Fire

This chapter is not a comprehensive list of all friction fire methods. There are many types of friction fire techniques, and many are best utilized in the specific region they were created in (e.g., fire thong, fire plough, fire saw). The bow drill is one of the most common forms of fiction fire and one of the most reliable. There are a variety of resources that can be used to build a bow drill kit. There are different bow drill variations, and some are more consistent than others (e.g., The Egyptian bow drill, Prusik Knot bow drill, and Hand Tensioned bow drill). The Egyptian bow drill is one of the best and most versatile variations. It is one of the few forms of the bow drill that allows for weaker cordage.

Strengths: Almost any dry, softwood will work to construct a bow drill kit.
Weakness: The bow drill requires relatively strong cordage and requires a lot of practice to develop the skill.
Materials: The bow drill consists of a spindle, socket, fireboard, bow and cordage.

Figure 5. Egyptian Bow Drill. This figure illustrates the elements of an Egyptian bow drill.

Hand Drill
Primitive Fire

The hand drill is one of the simplest forms of friction fire. It has relatively few moving parts but requires specific low ignition materials. Constant speed is more critical than downward pressure. If too much pressure is applied, the spindle can burn through the fireboard. Too much pressure increases the amount of friction between the spindle and fireboard. Too much friction makes it more challenging to get the speed needed to produce an ember (e.g., coal). The increased friction can also result in blistering of the hands. There are several hand drills and modifications to traditional designs (e.g., Traditional, Thumb Loop and Gas Pedal Hand Drill).

Strengths: The hand drill is easy to assemble and has few moving parts. If a person has the right materials, it quickly produces an ember.
Weakness: The hand drill is by the resources required. It requires a straight spindle and low ignition woods. Attempting the hand drill with the wrong resources can result in blistered hands. If a person is not skilled with the hand drill technique, it requires muscular endurance to produce an ember.
Materials: It is necessary to make a spindle and fireboard to construct a hand drill kit. It is best if the spindle and fireboard are made from the same material. A dry yucca stalk is one of the best resources for a hand drill spindle and fireboard. Yucca has a low ignition point and catches fire quickly.

Figure 6. Thumb Loop Hand Drill. This figure illustrates the elements of a Thumb Loop Hand Drill.

Fire Roll
Primitive Fire

The fire roll is a relatively easy friction fire method to teach and one of the easiest methods to learn. It requires fibers that are sufficiently durable to make it through the rolling process. The fibers must be combustible and have a low ignition point. The fire roll requires a dry powder placed in the center of the roll. The powder retains heat from friction resulting in the combustion of the fibers. Most of the powders used are not flammable (e.g., wood ash and handwarmer material) and are insulators that hold heat inside the fire roll. There are several fire roll variations, all with different fibers and internal powder (e.g., insulator). Some of the most popular variations are the Coconut Husk Fire Roll, Yucca Fire Roll and Cotton Fire Roll. The Cotton Fire Roll is the preferred method to teach when introducing the skill to students. It is by far the easiest of all methods.

Strengths: The fire roll has few moving parts and is easy to assemble.
Weakness: The fire roll is limited by the fibers needed to hold the powder internal. Finding natural fibers that are durable enough and have a low ignition temperature is problematic in some environments
Materials: The fire roll requires low ignition temperature and two flat surfaces to roll the bundle to ignition.

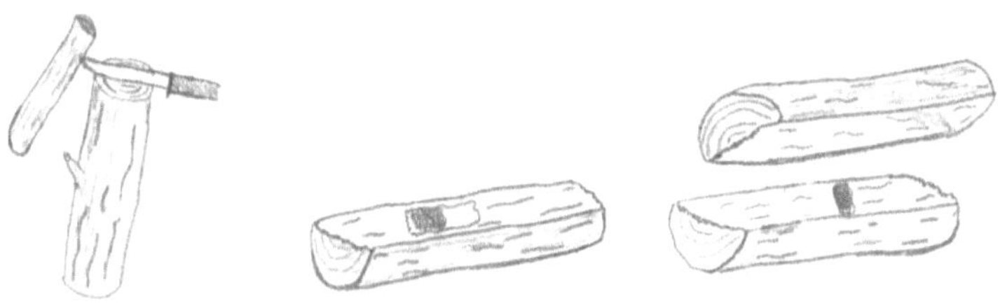

Figure 7. Fire Roll. This figure illustrates the elements of a fire roll.

Tinder Bundle
Primitive Fire

Making an ember is only half the battle when making a primitive fire. A good tinder bundle is essential to make sure the ember turns into a flame. Tinder bundles can be made from grass, leaves, bark, etc. All good tinder bundles are made from a dry material with a lot of surface area. It may be necessary to get shavings from the inner portions of dead limbs to gather enough dry resources in wet environments. Making matchsticks (e.g., feather sticks) and gathering enough dry kindling is also extremely useful when transferring the tinder bundle to start the fire.

Materials: Fat Wood (e.g., lighter knot, fat lighter, lighter wood, pine knot, heart pine) and other naturally flammable materials are useful resources that act as ember/coal extenders in the center of a tinder bundle. Other natural resources that act as ember extenders are tinder fungus, wood shavings, extra coal dust, cedar bark and sawdust. The center of the tinder bundle should act to extend the ember and should be at least the size of a golf ball. The ember extender should be surrounded by several inches of material with as much surface area as possible The outer material can be larger leaves and twigs. The tinder bundle should resemble a large bird's nest.

Figure 8. Tinder Bundle. This figure illustrates the elements of a tinder bundle.

Fire
Primitive Fire

There are several methods of making a fire. Fire stacking options are based on the situation and needs of the person. The most common fire design utilizes a Teepee structure. The Teepee structure is perfect when starting a fire due to the wood's forty-five-degree angle and airflow. Forty-five degrees is the perfect angle for the fire to burn upwards to catch other limbs on fire. The Teepee design also allows adequate airflow to speed up the burning process. Other stacking options change the fire's efficiency (e.g., Log Cabin, Platform, Star, Lean-To, etc.) Eventually, the logs will fall inward, and other stacking options can be used. The Teepee fire should be the first step when making primitive fires.

Materials: To build a primitive fire, a person needs a tinder bundle, twigs, sticks, small limbs and logs. The tinder bundle can be placed on the ground with dry leaves twigs placed over it at a forty-five-degree angle. It is essential at this stage not to smother the fire. Once the twigs have caught on fire, they can be covered with sticks at a forty-five-degree angle. Once the sticks have caught, they can be covered with small logs at forty-five-degree angles.

Figure 9. Primitive Fire. This figure illustrates two examples of primitive fire structures.

Seep Well
Primitive Water Treatment

A seep or sip well is a good option if there is no other alternative to filter the available water source. It is important to be two to three feet away from the water source to filter the water adequately. A seep well is also dependent upon the type of soil present. It requires soil that is porous enough for water to flow from the source to the well's location. Soil that contains a lot of clay will not allow the water to filter through to fill the well.

Strengths: A seep well required no fire, easy to make, and requires no tools.
Weakness: Filtering does not eliminate bacteria, viruses, pesticides or heavy metals.
Materials: A seep well requires porous soil and digging tool.

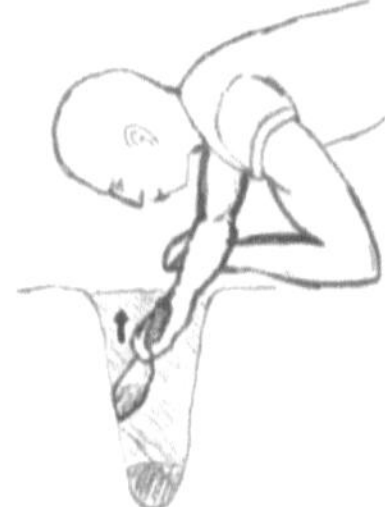 

Figure 10. Seep Well. This figure illustrates the elements of a seep well.

Charcoal Filter
Primitive Water Treatment

A carbon filter can be made from natural resources. The bark of a green limb, clay or large piece of bamboo can contain the filter ingredients. Carbon, gravel and nonpoisonous leaves can be used for the filter itself. The charcoal needs to be crushed and layered along with the gravel and leaves. It is best to have six inches or more of the charcoal for the water to pass through. Place the leaves at the bottom-most layer and then add the gravel. After the gravel, add charcoal and then another layer of gravel followed by leaves. The leaves prevent the charcoal and gravel from being eroded out of the filter by the flowing water.

Strengths: The filter can be made from natural resources and can be quickly made.
Weakness: Primitive filters do not eliminate bacteria, viruses, pesticides or heavy metals. Primitive filters require charcoal or fire to produce charcoal.
Materials: The charcoal filter requires fresh bark, grasses, clay or a large bamboo piece for the container. The materials used to filter the water include charcoal, gravel and nonpoisonous leaves.

Figure 11. Charcoal Filter. This figure illustrates the elements of charcoal filters.

Boiling Water
Primitive Water Treatment

Boiling is one of the most common ways to treat water to make it safe to drink. Many experts give various lengths of time for boiling needed to kill all pathogens. An excellent way to verify if the water is safe to drink is the adage, "Big bubbles, no troubles". The statement refers to producing bubbles during boiling. Bringing water to a rolling boil eliminates any pathogens that might cause gastrointestinal distress. Natural containers can be made out of wood, clay or bamboo. For flammable containers, hot rocks can be used to boil the water. Ground wells lined with clay can also be used in conjunction with hot rocks for boiling.

Strengths: Boiling kills all pathogens.
Weakness: Boiling does not eliminate pesticides or heavy metals. It also takes time to create a container and boil the water. The boiling process requires fire, and much of the water may be lost through evaporation.
Materials: Wood, bamboo or holes lined with clay can be used in conjunction with hot rocks to boil water.

Figure 12. Boiling Water. This figure illustrates two primitive methods of boiling water.

Distilling Water
Primitive Water Treatment

Distillation is the only method of treating water that eliminates all pathogens, heavy metals and pesticides. If a person has to distil their water, it is necessary to have some food to replace lost electrolytes. Some locations may have electrolytes in the soil, such as animal salt licks or saltwater. Without electrolytes, cells can't function properly, and people can die from water intoxication (i.e. hyponatremia). Most locations in the world have sufficient trash to make a distillery. A branch made from softwood can also be hollowed out to make a tube for distillation. The branch will need to have at least a forty-five-degree bend to prevent the container's water from being forced out during boiling. Cordage (i.e., clove hitches followed by half hitches) can be used to bind the limb back together, and leaves or clay can be used to seal the cracks. The limb can also be covered by wet sand or soil to help contain the tube's steam.

Strengths: Distilling water eliminates all contaminates.
Weakness: A distillation device is difficult and time-consuming to make. Distillation eliminates electrolytes from water, and some methods require fire for evaporation to occur.
Materials: To distil water using primitive means requires a clay container, bamboo or hollow limb.

Figure 13. Distilling Water. This figure illustrates two methods of distillation.

Edible Plants
Food

The information in this book is not a comprehensive list of all edible plants. The following plants can either be found all year in Texas, found the majority of the year, can be stored for long periods or found worldwide. Plants that are edible but do not have the nutritional or medicinal value are not listed (e.g., Pony's Foot, Lizards Tail, Milkweed, etc.). There are hundreds of edible plants found in Texas, and this book highlights some of the most common in Texas. For more information on edible and medicinal plants native to Texas, refer to Common Edible and Medicinal Plants of Texas. It is available on Amazon as an eBook or in print. The following plants are taught in a college-level Wilderness Survival class. The Texas map provides a visual example of the estimated range of the plant. The QR code provides a link to a playlist that covers essential information. The video provides greater detail than can be acquired through reading and looking at illustrations.

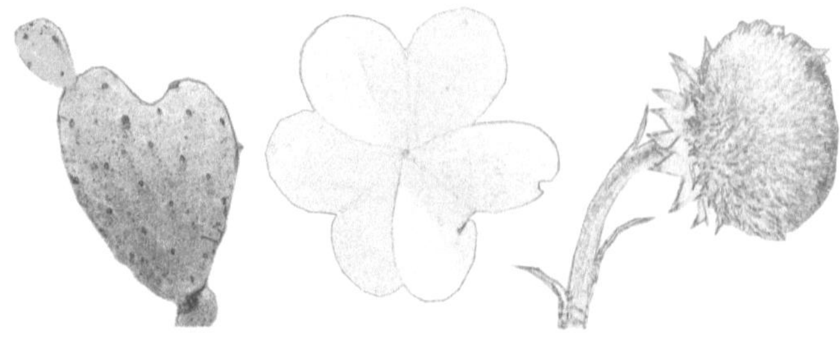

Figure 14. Edible Plants. This figure illustrates common edible plants found in Texas. Prickly Pear, Wood Sorrel and Milk Thistle are edible and found in most parts of Texas.

Acorn
Quercus spp.

Other Names: White Oak, Red Oak, Live Oak, Bur Oak, Blackjack Oak, Chinkapin Oak.
What to Use: The oak nut.
When to Find: Fall.
Where to Find: Most wooded areas in Texas.
How to Use: Tannins must be washed out of the acorn to make them edible. Cold washing involves soaking the shelled acorn nut in several changes of water until the tannins leach out. Cold washing preserves the starch in the flour but takes time. Boiling is a faster process and allows the acorns to be converted to flour on demand. If the acorns cool before all the tannic acid is removed, it can be more challenging to remove the remaining tannic acid (Vorderbruggen, Acorn - Oak, 2019).
Survival Uses: Acorns are excellent survival food. They can be stored unshelled in a cool, dry place or processed into flour and stored for months. Acorns were a staple of Native Americans and provided a consistent primary macronutrient source (e.g., fats, proteins, and carbohydrates).
Dangers: Tannic acid can be harmful in large quantities.

Figure 15. Bur Oak Acorn (Quercus macrocarpa). Found in Live Oak, Texas, on November 6th, 2018.

Figure 16. Bur Oak Acorn (Quercus macrocarpa). Found in Live Oak, Texas, on November 6th, 2018.

Amaranth
Amaranthus spp.

Other Names: Pigweed, Carelessweed, Quelites, Bledo.
What to Use: Young leaves and seeds.
When to Find: Summer for young leaves and late summer or Fall for seeds.
Where to Find: Disturbed soil and ditches.
How to Use: The leaves must be harvested when the plant is young. Once the plant ages, the leaves are too fibrous to eat. The young leaves can be eaten raw or cooked. The seeds will only develop if there are sufficient rains during the summer. The seeds can be eaten raw or ground into flour. The seeds have been used as a grain by Native Americans for thousands of years (Kane 2017, 9).
Survival Uses: Amaranth is an excellent source for macronutrients, and the grain is excellent survival food. Grains can be stored for long periods and can be used for long term survival. It is necessary to wind winnow the grains to separate the seed from the chaff.
Dangers: None.

Figure 17. Amaranth (Amaranthus spp.). Found on the Brazos River, Texas, on March 22nd, 2017.

Figure 18. Amaranth (Amaranthus spp.). Found on the Brazos River, Texas, on March 22nd, 2017.

Bamboo
Arundinaria gigantean

Other Names: Rivercane.
What to Use: Young shoots and seeds.
When to Find: Spring and early summer.
Where to Find: Streams, rivers, ponds or lakes.
How to Use: Once the new bamboo spouts, it can easily be collected. The sprouts can be eaten raw or cooked and can be mixed with other plants in a salad. Bamboo is not nutrient-dense, but it has significant B vitamins, which helps convert food to fuel. Examine the bamboo for brown to purplish powder before eating. Bamboo is prone to contamination by the deadly Ergot fungus. (Vorderbruggen, Bamboo, 2018).
Survival Uses: Bamboo is one of the most useful plants for survival. It can be used as a bamboo fire saw to create primitive friction fire. Green bamboo can be used as a container and often contains water inside that has been filtered and is safe to drink. Bamboo can be used to build shelters and various tools. Overall, it is one of the most useful survival plants.
Dangers: Ergot fungus can contaminate the plant.

Figure 19. Bamboo (Arundinaria gigantean).
Found in Live Oak, Texas, on June 10th, 2017.

Figure 20. Bamboo (Arundinaria gigantean).
Found in Live Oak, Texas, on June 10th, 2017.

Bastard Cabbage
Brassica, Rapistrum and Sinapis spp.

Other Names: Wild Mustard, Turnipweed.
What to Use: Young leaves, seeds pods, flowers and flower buds.
When to Find: Fall through early summer.
Where to Find: Disturbed areas, ditches and fields.
How to Use: Wild mustard is considered cruciferous and is in the same family as cabbage, cauliflower, broccoli, turnips, kale, kohlrabi, wasabi, peppergrass and Shepherd's purse. It is best to harvest the young leaves before the leaves become bitter and fibrous. The seeds can be ground, mixed with vinegar and used to make mustard. A small percentage of the population may be allergic to wild mustard (Kane 2017, 11).
Survival Uses: Bastard cabbage is an excellent source of nutrition during the winter. When most nutritious plants have died, wild mustards start growing. Mustards can be foraged and used for short-term survival or canned for long-term survival. Due to their low acid content, they must be pickled for long-term storage.
Dangers: A small percentage of the population may be allergic to wild mustard.

Figure 21. Bastard Cabbage (Rapistrum rugosum). Found in Live Oak, Texas, on April 28th, 2017.

Figure 22. Bastard Cabbage (Rapistrum rugosum). Found in Live Oak, Texas, on April 28th, 2017.

Black Walnut
Juglans nigra

Other Names: Eastern Black Walnut, Green Walnut, Jupiter's Nuts.
What to Use: Nuts and sap.
When to Find: Fall.
Where to Find: Fields and forest.
How to Use: Black Walnut contains high amounts of macronutrients (e.g., protein, fats and carbohydrates). The unshelled nuts can last a long time in storage if they are kept dry. A hammer or hatchet may be necessary during the shelling. Once shelled, the nut is much smaller than the traditional English walnut (Vorderbruggen, Black Walnut, 2019). All species of walnut (e.g., Juglans spp.) produce sap that can be boiled down into valuable syrup (Hammonds, 2019).
Survival Uses: The husk also contains juglones that can poison fish and cause them to float to the surface. Native American used the crushed husk to poison fish to make them easy to gather. The juice from the green husk has also been used to treat ringworm (Vorderbruggen, Black Walnut, 2019).
Dangers: The shell will stain fingers, juglones will poison fish and neighbouring plants.

Figure 23. Black Walnut (Juglans nigra).
Found in Anna, Texas, on January 27th, 2018.

Figure 24. Black Walnut (Juglans nigra).
Found in Anna, Texas, on January 27th, 2018.

Blackberry
Rubus argutus

Other Names: Sawtooth Blackberry, Southern Blackberry, Highbush Blackberry.
What to Use: Berries, leaves, and flowers.
When to Find: Spring and early summer.
Where to Find: Ditches, borders of fields and woods.
How to Use: Blackberries are often confused with dewberries but are much larger and not as sweet. The berries can be eaten raw or stored for later use. The berries can be made into jelly, jam or fermented into wine. The young leaves and flowers can be used to make tea (Kane 2017, 13).
Survival Uses: Like many berries, blackberries are seasonal and need to be processed to be stored. They can be made into juice, syrup, jelly, jam, preserves and canned for long-term storage. They can also be dried if canning is not an option. Fermentation allows the juice to be converted to wine, which then can be bottled for long-term storage (Kane 2017, 13).
Dangers: Thorns.

Figure 25. Blackberry (Rubus spp.).
Found in Anna, Texas, on May 5th, 2018.

Figure 26. Blackberry (Rubus spp.).
Found in Anna, Texas, on May 5th, 2018.

Cactus-Prickly Pear
Opuntia spp.

Other Names: Tuna (fruit), Sabra, Nopal, Nopales.
What to Use: Fruits and young pads.
When to Find: All year.
Where to Find: Sunny fields and fence lines.
How to Use: Prickly Pear and Cow's Tongue are very similar, vary slightly in appearance, but have similar uses. The young pads typically grow in the spring, but in Texas, the fruit can be found in different growth stages all year around. The young pads can be eaten raw, cooked but are best when boiled for about 10 minutes. The fruits can be made into juices, jellies or fermented into wine. It is essential to remove the tiny thorns called glochids from the fruits and pads. The easiest way to remove glochids is to burn them off over an open flame (Tull, 1999).
Survival Uses: Prickly Pear is one of the best plants for short-term and long-term survival. Some part of the plant is available at all times of the year. The fruits can easily be made into jelly or fermented into wine to provide a source of calories for long-term survival.
Dangers: Glochids can be harmful if swallowed. A small percentage of people are allergic to cactus-based foods.

Figure 27. Prickly Pear Cactus (Opuntia ellisiana).
Found in Live Oak, Texas, on September 29th, 2018.

Figure 28. Prickly Pear Cactus (Opuntia ellisiana).
Found in Live Oak, Texas, on September 29th, 2018.

Carrot - Wild
Daucus carota

Other Names: Bird's Nest, Bishop's Lace, Queen Anne's Lace.
What to Use: Young roots, young stems and seeds.
When to Find: The young roots are found in the spring, the seeds are found in the late summer and fall.
Where to Find: Fields and ditches.
How to Use: The young root is woody and best used to flavor soups and then removed. Wild Carrot can be easily confused with the highly toxic Hemlock plant. Wild Carrot will have a single stalk with a single flat flower or seed cluster at the top. If the root smells like a carrot, it is a wild carrot, and if the root smells terrible, it is most likely Water Hemlock. If the sap from Water Hemlock gets into a person's eye, it can cause blindness. It takes very little ingested Water Hemlock to kill a human. It is important to know how identify both plants before eating Wild Carrot (Vorderbruggen, Queen Anne's Lace/Wild Carrot, 2018).
Survival Uses: The seeds can be used in the same manner as dill seeds as a pickling spice. The young roots can also be pickled for long-term survival.
Dangers: Wild Carrot can be easily confused with the highly toxic Hemlock plant.

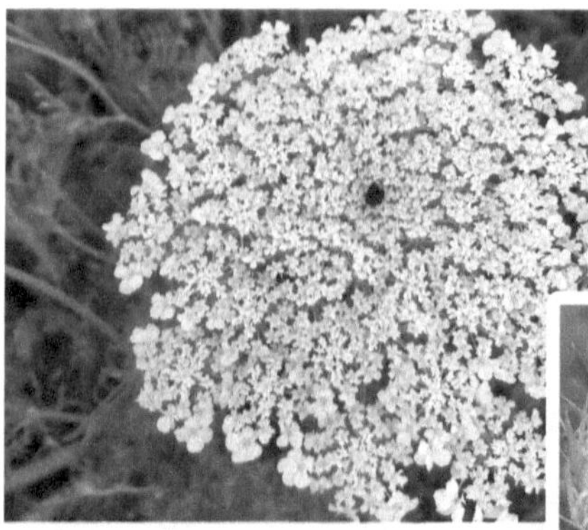

Figure 29. Wild Carrot (Daucus carota).
Found in Anna, Texas, on April 28th, 2017.

Figure 30. Wild Carrot (Daucus carota).
Found in Anna, Texas, on April 28th, 2017.

Cattails
Typha latifolia

Other Names: Bullrush, Espadilla, Punks, Corn Dog Grass, Swamp Sausage, Water Sausage.
What to Use: Roots, new shoots, immature punk.
When to Find: Roots in the winter, new shoots and punk in the spring.
Where to Find: Creeks, ponds, water-filled ditches.
How to Use: Cattail can be found worldwide and is one of the best-known survival foods. Almost every part of the plant is edible at some point in the year. It is best to harvest the cattail in early spring when the new shoots start to sprout from the root. The root is best harvested in the winter and easy to cook for consumption. The male portion of the flower is eaten like corn on the cob. The pollen can be collected in the spring and used as flour. Make sure to cook any part of the plant in contact with water to kill any waterborne pathogens (Kane 2017, 15).
Survival Uses: The dry stalk from the cattail can be used as a hand drill and arrow. The fluffy seed pods can be used as insulation or in a tinder bundle to make fire. All portions of the cattail can be canned, and the flour can be stored in a dry place for long-term survival.
Dangers: Possible contamination from waterborne pathogens.

Figure 31. Cattail (Typha latifolia). Found in Live Oak, Texas, on May 11th, 2017.

Figure 32. Cattail (Typha latifolia). Found in Live Oak, Texas, on May 11th, 2017.

Dandelion
Taraxacum officinale

Other Names: Blow Ball, Cankerwort, Cochet, Lion's Tooth, Priest's Crown, Swine Snout.
What to Use: All parts.
When to Find: Spring and early summer.
Where to Find: Fields, brushland, and yards.
How to Use: Dandelion is another superfood found all year in Texas. It has assorted protein, vitamins and minerals. It has nutritional and medicinal qualities. Dandelion can be eaten raw, cooked or baked. The root should be roasted and ground to the consistency of coffee grounds. The flowers of dandelion can be boiled and made into tea. They can also be fermented into wine. Pickling, boiling, or applying a vinegar-based salad dressing will reduce the leaves' bitterness (Vorderbruggen, Dandelion, 2019).
Survival Uses: Dandelion is a nutrient-rich food that can be eaten for short-term survival. All parts of the plant are edible and can be dried, pickled or canned for long-term storage.
Dangers: None.

Figure 33. Dandelion (Taraxacum officinale). Found in Live Oak, Texas, on February 13th, 2017.

Figure 34. Dandelion (Taraxacum officinale). Found in Live Oak, Texas, on February 13th, 2017.

Dewberry
Rubus spp.

Other Names: Falling Dewberry, Garden Dewberry, Northern and Southern Dewberry.
What to Use: Fruits and leaves.
When to Find: Spring an summer.
Where to Find: Fields, disturbed areas, sunny and wooded areas.
How to Use: Dewberry is similar to blackberry in nutrition and use. The berry is a smaller, sweeter version of blackberry. The fruits can be eaten raw, made into jelly, jam or fermented into a wine. The young leaves can be steeped and made into tea. For more information about uses, refer to blackberry (Kane 2017, 19).
Survival Uses: The berries can be eaten raw or cooked for short-term survival. The berries can also be fermented or canned for long-term survival. The berries are calorically dense and nutrient-rich and can provide substantial calories for short-term and long-term survival.
Dangers: Thorns.

Figure 35. Dewberry (Rubus spp.).
Found in Live Oak, Texas, on April 26th, 2017.

Figure 36. Dewberry (Rubus spp.).
Found in Live Oak, Texas, on April 26th, 2017.

Dock
Rumex spp.

Other Names: Curled Dock, Curly Dock, Yellow Dock, Pale Dock, Amamastia Dock.
What to Use: Young leaves and seeds.
When to Find: Spring and summer.
Where to Find: Fields, disturbed areas, ditches, rivers and ponds.
How to Use: The seeds, young leaves, and roots can be eaten. The young leaves are high in nutrients, and the seeds can be ground into flour. A medicinal tea can be made from boiling the root. The young leaves are tender enough to eat raw, but the older leaves need to be boiled to make them more palatable. The leaves also contain oxalic acid and must be cooked to eat in large quantities. Too much oxalic acid can result in kidney stones in some individuals (Kane 2017, 20).
Survival Uses: The leaves can be eaten raw in small quantities or cooked for short-term survival. The leaves can be pickled or canned for later use. The seeds are a great source of protein and can be stored in a dry place for long-term survival.
Dangers: The leaves also contain oxalic acid and need to be cooked before eating.

Figure 37. Dock (Rumex crispus).
Found in Live Oak, Texas, on March 13th, 2017.

Figure 38. Dock (Rumex crispus).
Found in Live Oak, Texas, on March 13th, 2017.

Duckweed
Spirodela polyrhiza, Lemna minor

Other Names: Water Lens, Grains De Grenouille, Herbe Aux Canards, Ranouillie.
What to Use: The whole plant.
When to Find: Summer.
Where to Find: Ponds and lakes.
How to Use: Duckweed is high in protein to increase the protein content of other foods. Many farmers and ranchers use it to increase the protein content in their feed for livestock. Duckweed can be dried and then added to other food sources. It grows on lakes or still ponds throughout the summer and grows so fast it can completely cover a water source. It can also be used as an insect repellent (Vorderbruggen, Duckweed, 2018).
Survival Uses: Duckweed can be eaten raw or cooked for short-term survival. It can be pickled or dried for later use and long-term survival. Due to the high protein content, it can be used as a supplement for other plant sources.
Dangers: Cook duckweed before eating to prevent exposure to waterborne pathogens.

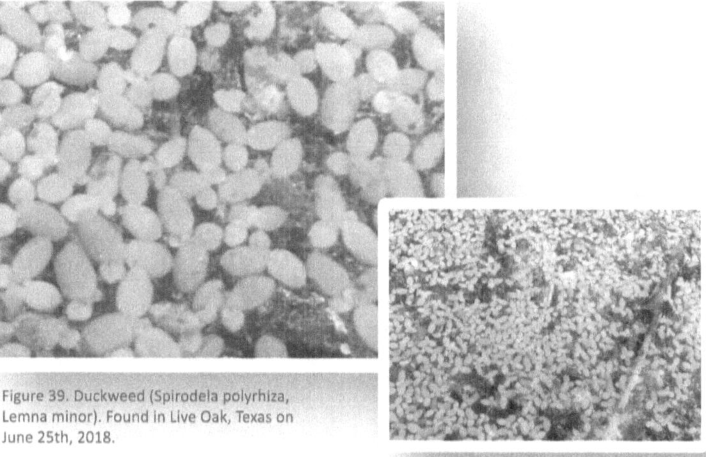

Figure 39. Duckweed (Spirodela polyrhiza, Lemna minor). Found in Live Oak, Texas on June 25th, 2018.

Figure 40. Duckweed (Spirodela polyrhiza, Lemna minor). Found in Live Oak, Texas on June 25th, 2018.

Elderberry
Sambucus nigra. canadensis, S. mexicana

Other Names: Elder, American Black Elderberry, Common Elder.
What to Use: Ripe berries.
When to Find: Late summer and early fall.
Where to Find: Banks of wooded creeks, rivers, and streams.
How to Use: Elderberry are small trees that grow six to twelve feet tall and will continue to flower throughout the summer. The berries can be eaten raw, but it is best to dry or cook the berries to remove the oil that gives them a foul taste. Only harvest the ripe berries, unripe berries can be toxic. The berries can be made into jams, jellies, and pies or fermented into a wine. Do not confuse the elderberry with pokeweed or other similar toxic berries. All other parts of the elderberry bush are poisonous. The berries have a rich history of medicinal uses and nutritional benefits (Kane 2017, 22).
Survival Uses: The berries can be eaten raw or cooked for short-term survival. Berries can also be canned, fermented or dried for long-term survival. The elderberry tree trunk is a good source of straight hand and bow drill spindles for primitive fire-making.
Dangers: Use the ripe berries only, all other parts of the plant are poisonous.

Figure 41. Elderberry (Sambucus Canadensis). Found in Anna, Texas, on June 10th, 2017.

Figure 42. Elderberry (Sambucus Canadensis). Found in Anna, Texas, on June 10th, 2017.

Grapes
Vitis spp.

Other Names: Mustang Grapes, Muscadine Grapes, Frost Grapes.
What to Use: Fruits, leaves, young tendrils and seeds.
When to Find: Late summer and early fall.
Where to Find: Woods and fence lines.
How to Use: There are three types of wild grapes in Texas, but the two most commonly used are Mustang and Muscadine. Muscadine typically grows in the woods in the upper canopy of the trees. Mustang grape vines are more commonly found growing in fence rows and on small trees in South and Central Texas. The leaves, grapes and young tendrils can be eaten. The white powder that grows on Mustang grapes' leaves is yeast and can be fermented into wine and making bread. Frost grapes are small and ripe after the first frost. Grapes can be made into a jelly, jam, dried into raisins or ferment into wine. The seeds can be crushed to extract the oil (Tull, 1999).
Survival Uses: Wild grapes can be eaten raw for short-term survival or made into jelly, jam, fermented into wine or dried into raisins for long-term storage.
Dangers: Mustang grapes are very acidic.

Figure 43. Mustang Grapes (Vitis mustangensis). Found in Pleasanton, Texas, on June 23rd, 2018.

Figure 44. Frost Grapes (Vitis vulpina). Found in Anna, Texas, on August 26th, 2018.

Greenbrier
Smilax spp.

Other Names: Catbriar, Greenbriar.
What to Use: Tendrils, roots, berries and leaves.
When to Find: All year.
Where to Find: Woods and fence lines.
How to Use: Parts of the plant can be found anytime of the year. The root is available all year, but it is best to harvest it in the spring. The root can be sliced and dried. Once dry, it can be crumbled into a pot of water and the fibers will float to the top while the starch will sink to the bottom. The tendrils start developing in early March in South Texas. The first 12 inches is soft enough to eat. In late fall and winter, the berries will develop, and the seed's outer covering is edible (Vorderbruggen, Greenbriar, 2018).
Survival Uses: Due to the plant's availability and starch content of the root, Greenbriar is an excellent resource for short-term and long-term survival. The tendrils can be eaten raw or pickled, and the root can be dried and made into flour for long-term survival. The berries can be made into jelly or fermented into wine.
Dangers: Thorns.

Figure 45. Greenbrier (Smilax spp).
Found in Live Oak, Texas, on March 22nd, 2017.

Figure 46. Greenbrier (Smilax spp).
Found in Live Oak, Texas, on March 22nd, 2017.

Ground Cherry
Physalis spp.

Other Names: Cape Gooseberry, Golden Berry, Pichuberry, Inca Berry, Poha Berry.
What to Use: Berries.
When to Find: Summer and late fall depending on the species.
Where to Find: Woods, shaded areas, open fields and fence lines.
How to Use: Ground Cherries are related to the tomato, tomatillo, black nightshade and are in the nightshade family. It is very important not to eat the fruit until it has fully ripened. The unripe fruit will have a small amount of toxic compounds that can cause upset stomach, vomiting and diarrhea. The fruits will usually fall from the plant before ripening and can be left in open sunlight to fully ripen. The fruit will change from yellow to orange after it has ripened, some species will be a dark orange-red in color. The plant has a sweet, tomato-tomatillo like taste (Kane 2017, 25).
Survival Uses: The fruits can be eaten raw or cooked for short-term survival. Ground cherries can be dried or made into salsa and canned for long-term storage. The plants are nutrient dense and a great source of food for survival.
Dangers: Berries that have not ripened can cause an upset stomach, vomiting and diarrhea.

Figure 47. Ground Cherry (Physalis species).
Found in Anna, Texas on April 30th, 2017.

Figure 48. Ground Cherry (Physalis species).
Found in Anna, Texas on June 28th, 2017.

Henbit
Lamium amplexicaule

Other Names: Henbit Dead Nettle, Common Henbit, Greater Henbit.
What to Use: Leaves, stems, flowers.
When to Find: Winter and spring.
Where to Find: Fields, yards, sunny areas.
How to Use: One of the most common edible plants during the winter, Henbit will usually sprout after the first freeze. It can be easily identified by the small purple flowers that grow on the top of the plant. The entire plant is edible and can be eaten raw, cooked or mixed into a salad with other wild edibles. It is commonly confused with Dead Nettle (Lamium purpureum), which is also edible but not nutritious. It has a similar taste to celery with a mildly peppery taste (Vorderbruggen, Henbit, 2018).
Survival Uses: Henbit can be eaten raw or cooked making it is a good source of food for short-term survival. It can also be canned or pickled for long-term storage. Henbit can be dried and ground into a spice to flavor foods. It is one of the most common edible plants that grow during the winter in Texas.
Dangers: None.

Figure 49. Henbit (Lamium amplexicaule).
Found in Live Oak, Texas, on December 31st, 2018.

Figure 50. Henbit (Lamium amplexicaule).
Found in Live Oak, Texas, on January 13th, 2019.

Lamb's Quarter
Chenopodium album

Other Names: Melde, Goosefoot, Fat-Hen.
What to Use: Leaves and young stems.
When to Find: Spring, summer, fall.
Where to Find: Disturbed areas and fields.
How to Use: Lamb's Quarter should be harvested when the leaves are young. Lamb's Quarter can be confused with Silverleaf Nightshade, especially when the plants are still young. Silverleaf Nightshade will develop a large purple flower with yellow in the center of the flower around the stamen. Lamb's Quarter develops small flowers, but they are often confused with small seeds due to their size. The leaves are a good spinach substitute (Boutenko, Wild Edibles, 2013).
Survival Uses: The leaves and young stems can be eaten raw or cooked for short-term survival. The leaves and young stems can be pickled or dried for long-term use. The roots can be crushed to extract a soap substitute (Plants For A Future, Chenopodium album - L., 2019).
Dangers: Similar appearance to the toxic silverleaf nightshade.

Figure 51. Lamb's Quarter (Chenopodium album). Found in Live Oak, Texas, on February 22nd, 2019.

Figure 52. Lamb's Quarter (Chenopodium album). Found in Live Oak, Texas, on February 22nd, 2019.

Mulberry
Morus microphylla

Other Names: Texas Mulberry, Littleleaf Mulberry, Mountain Mulberry, Mexican Mulberry, Dwarf Mulberry.
What to Use: Berries, young leaves, inner bark.
When to Find: Spring and summer.
Where to Find: Woods, creek banks, yards.
How to Use: The mulberry tree grows throughout Texas, normally near a water source. The leaves, inner bark and berries are edible. The leaves can be eaten raw or added to a salad. The berries are ripe when they are easily plucked from the tree. A ripe berry will range from red to purple when ripe and an excellent source of antioxidants and carbohydrates. The berries are eaten raw, made into jelly, jam, or fermented into wine (Vorderbruggen, Mulberry, 2019).
Survival Uses: The berries are eaten raw or cooked for short-term survival. The berries can be made into jelly, jam or fermented into wine for long-term storage.
Dangers: None.

Figure 53. Mulberry (Morus microphylla).
Found in Live Oak, Texas, on April 4th, 2017.

Figure 54. Mulberry (Morus microphylla).
Found in Live Oak, Texas, on April 4th, 2017.

Onion-Wild
Allium species

Other Names: Prairie Onion, Plains Onion, Canada Onion, Canadian Garlic, Wild Garlic, Meadow Garlic.
What to Use: All parts of the plant.
When to Find: Winter until the end of summer.
Where to Find: Borders of rivers, lakes, streams and flooded areas.
How to Use: The entire plant can be used as a domestic onion. The older wild onion plants can become tough with age and it may be necessary to boil them before eating. The plant can be dried or canned for later use. Wild Onion is often confused with the mildly toxic Crow's Poison. The easiest way to differentiate between the two plants is to crush a small sample. If it smells like onion or garlic, it is Wild Onion. Crow's Poison will smell like grass (Kane 2017, 61).
Survival Uses: Wild Onion can be found most of the year and can be eaten raw or cooked for short-term survival. The plant can be dried or canned for long-term storage.
Dangers: Do not be confused with the similarity to mildly toxic Crow's Poison.

Figure 55. Wild Onion (Allium species).
Found in Live Oak, Texas, on February 8th, 2017.

Figure 56. Wild Onion (Allium species).
Found in Live Oak, Texas, on February 8th, 2017.

Palm
Many species

Other Names: Texas Sabal Palm, California Fan Palm, Dwarf Palmetto Palm, Queen Palm, Pindo Palm.
What to Use: Heart of palm, seeds, fruit, and sap.
When to Find: Depends on the type of palm.
Where to Find: Landscaping, rivers and beaches.
How to Use: Many species of palm fruits are made into jelly or fermented into wine. Many have seeds that can be pressed into palm oil that is good for cooking. The sap can also be utilized as a drink, wine or reduced down to a syrup. Harvesting the heart of palm will kill the tree, but the heart of palm can be collected any time of the year and is an excellent source of carbohydrates (Vorderbruggen, Palm - Texas Sabal, 2019).
Survival Uses: Palm fronds make excellent natural cordage for weaving and friction fire. They can be used as waterproof shingles for a shelter roof or fiber for a fire roll. The sap, fruits and heart of palm can be eaten raw or cooked for short-term survival. They sap, jelly, oil and heart of palm can be canned for long-term survival.
Dangers: None.

Figure 57. California Fan Palm (Washingtonia filifera). Found in Live Oak, Texas, on June 10th, 2020.

Figure 58. Texas Sabal Palm (Sabal Mexicana). Found in Live Oak, Texas, on November 10th, 2017.

Pecan
Carya illinoinensis

Other Names: Pecan Nut, Pecan Tree, Illinois Nut.
What to Use: Nut.
When to Find: Fall.
Where to Find: Woods, fields and fence lines.
How to Use: There are many species of pecan Texas. The most desirable pecans are the large, soft shell variety. They are easy to crack and have a larger nut inside them. The smaller, harder to crack species tend to contain more oil and can be easily pressed to extract the oil. All pecans are great survival foods, are calorically dense, and are an excellent protein and fat source (Kane 2017, 43). Milk can be made from the nut and can be used to thicken other foods. A tea can be made from the leaf (Plants For A Future, Carya illinoinensis - (Wangenh.)K. Koch., 2019).
Survival Uses: Pecans can be eaten raw or cooked for short-term survival. They can also be placed in a dry area for long-term storage.
Dangers: None.

Figure 59. Pecan (Carya illinoinensis).
Found in Anna, Texas, on November 12th, 2019.

Figure 60. Pecan (Carya illinoinensis).
Found in Anna, Texas, on November 12th, 2019.

Persimmon-Common
Diospyros virginiana

Other Names: American Persimmon, Virginian Persimmon, Simmon, Possumwood, Possum Apples, Sugar Plum.
What to Use: Fruit.
When to Find: Late fall.
Where to Find: Fence rows, tree lines and open fields.
How to Use: The Common Persimmon fruit is dark orange and is soft to the touch when ripe. Before ripening, the fruit is extremely astringent and will remove all moisture from a person's mouth. The ripe fruit can be eaten raw or used to make jelly, jams and fermented into wine. The fruit must be fully ripe before using it due to its astringent nature (Kane 2017, 45).
Survival Uses: The fruits can be eaten raw or cooked for short-term survival. They can be made into jellies, jams, and fermented into wine for long-term storage.
Dangers: Unripe fruit is extraordinarily astringent and will remove all moisture from a person's mouth.

Figure 61. Persimmon (Diospyros virginiana).
Found in Anna, Texas, on November 10th, 2018.

Figure 62. Persimmon (Diospyros virginiana).
Found in Anna, Texas, on November 10th, 2018.

Persimmon-Texas
Diospyros texana

Other Names: Mexican Persimmon, Black Persimmon, Chapote, Chapote Prieto.
What to Use: Ripe fruits.
When to Find: Summer.
Where to Find: Brushland and hill country.
How to Use: Texas Persimmon fruits turn dark purple when ripe and will easily fall off the tree when picked. When a person harvests the fruit, it is not ripe unless it can be easily pulled from the tree, regardless of color. The fruits should be soft to the touch and sweet. The seeds can often be seen in animal scat, indicating a Texas Persimmon is nearby. The fruits can be made into jelly, jam, preserve or fermented into wine (Kane 2017, 45).
Survival Uses: Ripe fruits can be eaten fresh for short-term survival. The fruits can be dried or made into jam, preserve or fermented into wine for long-term storage.
Dangers: Unripe fruit is exceptionally astringent and will remove all moisture from a person's mouth.

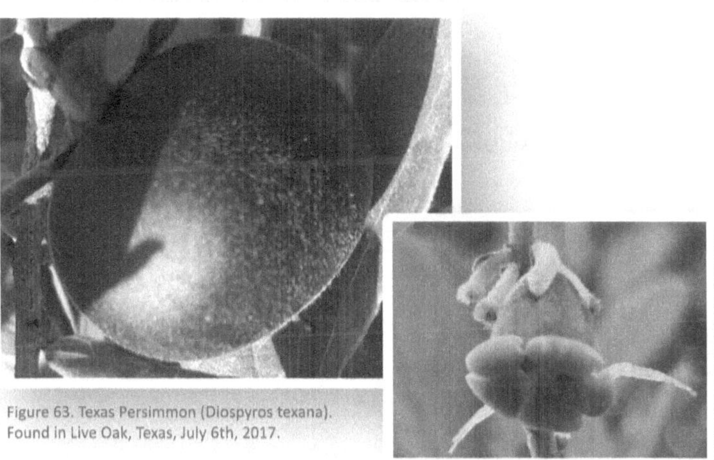

Figure 63. Texas Persimmon (Diospyros texana). Found in Live Oak, Texas, July 6th, 2017.

Figure 64. Texas Persimmon (Diospyros texana). Found in Live Oak, Texas, March 25th, 2017.

Pine Tree
Pinus taeda

Other Names: Loblolly Pine (Pinus taeda), White Pines (Pinus strobus), Yellow Pine (Multiple spp.)
Range: East Texas.
What to Use: Nuts, needles, inner bark, and pollen.
When to Find: Needles and the inner bark is found all year..
Where to Find: Forests, woods and landscaping.
How to Use: Pine needles are an excellent source of vitamin C. The inner bark of some pines are edible and can be used as a source of carbohydrate. Yellow pine pollen has been used as a testosterone supplement, Native American warriors used to consume it before battle to increase aggressiveness. The pine nuts can be hard to harvest once they fall to the ground because small animals will typically get to them first (Vorderbruggen, Loblolly Pine, 2020).
Survival Uses: Pine resin contains terpene that makes the hard resinous wood recovered from a dead pine tree (e.g., lighter knot, fatwood and pitchwood) highly flammable. Pine also makes an excellent friction fire source for fire boards and spindles. The sap can be used as pitch or glue when mixed with plant material and wood ash.
Dangers: Pregnant women should avoid due to phytoestrogens in needles.

Figure 65. Pine Tree (Pinus taeda).
Found in San Antonio, Texas on July 11th, 2020.

Figure 66. Pine Tree (Pinus taeda).
Found in San Antonio, Texas on July 11th, 2020.

Plantain
Plantago species

Other Names: Common Plantain, Cart Track Plant, White Man's Foot.
Range: All of Texas.
What to Use: Leaves, stalks, and seeds.
When to Find: Winter and early spring.
Where to Find: Open areas, yards and disturbed areas.
How to Use: Plantain is a medicinal plant that starts to grow at the end of winter. It has medicinal properties and has been used for thousands of years as an anti-inflammatory. The leaves can be boiled to make a tea to soothe sore throats and other digestive issues. The leaves can be crushed into a paste and placed on insect stings and rashes to reduce itching. The leaves can be eaten raw, but they are more palatable if they are cooked. When young, the seed heads can be eaten raw, and when they mature, the seeds can be harvested. The seeds can be eaten raw or ground into flour (Yetman 2012, 37).
Survival Uses: Plantain can be eaten raw or cooked for short-term survival. The seeds are high in B vitamins and can be stored in dry areas for long-term storage.
Dangers: None.

Figure 67. Plantain (Plantago spp.).
Found near Waco, Texas, on the Brazos River on March 6th, 2016.

Figure 68. Plantain (Plantago spp.).
Found near in Live Oak, Texas, on February 21st, 2017.

Plum-Wild
Prunus angustifolia and Prunus mexicana

Other Names: Cherokee Plum, Sand Plum, Mexican Plum, Bigtree Plum, Inch Plum.
Range: Most of Texas.
What to Use: Fruit.
When to Find: Summer and fall.
Where to Find: Fence lines and borders of woods.
How to Use: There are two main species of wild plum found in Texas. Chickasaw plums (Prunus angustifolia) are found in the early summer, and Mexican plums (Prunus Mexicana) are found in the fall. The fruit can be eaten raw or used to make jams or jellies. The seeds should not be eaten due to the low amount of cyanide they may contain. The outer covering of the fruit has a naturally occurring yeast can be used to make bread or ferment wines (Vorderbruggen, Plum - Wild, 2019).
Survival Uses: The fruits can be eaten raw or cooked for short-term survival. They can be dried, jellied or fermented into wine for long-term storage.
Dangers: The seeds should not be eaten due to the low amount of cyanide they may contain.

Figure 69. Chickasaw Plum (Prunus angustifolia). Found in Anna, Texas, on July 5th, 2018.

Figure 70. Mexican Plum (Prunus Mexicana). Found in Live Oak, Texas, on July 16th, 2017.

Pokeweed
Phytolacca americana L.

Other Names: American Pokeweed, Great Pokeweed, Pokeweed, Pokeberry, Red Ink Plant, Pigeonberry.
Range: North, Central and East Texas.
What to Use: Young shoots, leaves and berry juice.
When to Find: Spring and early summer.
Where to Find: Woods, fence lines, shady areas and brush piles.
How to Use: Pokeweed can be extremely toxic if not prepared correctly. It contains toxic alkaloids that must be boiled away. The young shoots and leaves must be harvested before any red coloring develops or not used. It is necessary to boil the leaves for five minutes and then drain the water to remove the poisonous alkaloids. Boiling must be done at least three times. The berries' seeds are highly toxic and cannot be eaten, but the juice from the berries can be made safe for consumption by boiling it. After boiling the juice, it can be made into a jam, jelly or fermented into wine. To ensure the berries are safe for consumption, it is best to cold wash (soak) the berries overnight before boiling (Vorderbruggen, Pokeweed/Poke Salat, 2019).
Survival Uses: Pokeweed must be adequately cooked before eating.
Dangers: All parts of the plant are poisonous without proper preparation.

Figure 71. Pokeweed (Phytolacca americana L).
Found in Anna, Texas, on August 5th, 2018.

Figure 72. Pokeweed (Phytolacca americana L).
Found in Anna, Texas, on August 5th, 2018.

Purslane
Portulaca oleracea

Other Names: Common Purslane, Verdolaga, Red Root, Pursley, Little Hogweed
Range: Most of Texas.
What to Use: Leaves and stems.
When to Find: Spring, summer and fall.
Where to Find: Yards and cracks of sidewalks.
How to Use: Purslane is cultivated worldwide accept in the United States and is one of the most nutritious survival foods. The stems and leaves can be eaten raw, boiled, fried or pickled. Purslane is sometimes confused with the toxic Spotted Spurge, but it can be easy to tell the two apart. Spotted Spurge is much smaller and will have a milky sap. Purslane will have clear sap, smooth stems that will vary from green to red. Purslane will have thick and plump leaves. Spotted Spurge stems will have small hairs but can be difficult to see due to the plant's size (Kane 2017, 48).
Survival Uses: The leaves and stems can be eaten raw or cooked for short-term survival. Both can be pickled or canned for long-term storage.
Dangers: Purslane resembles the toxic Spotted Spurge plant.

Figure 73. Purslane (Portulaca oleracea).
Found in Live Oak, Texas, on February 14th, 2017.

Figure 74. Purslane (Portulaca oleracea).
Found in Live Oak, Texas, on February 14th, 2017.

Rose
Rosa spp.

Other Names: Wild Rose.
Range: West, South, East, North and Central Texas.
What to Use: Flowers and hips.
When to Find: Fall.
Where to Find: Fence lines and borders of woods.
How to Use: Rose petals can be eaten raw or made into a jelly. Rose hips can also be eaten raw once the seeds are removed. The seeds inside the rose hips are covered in small hairs that can cause irritation to a person's throat if eaten. The rose hips can be made into jelly, jam, tea, or fermented into wine (Boutenko, Wild Edibles, 2013).
Survival Uses: The petals and hips can be eaten raw or cooked for short-term survival. Both can be made into jelly or fermented wine for long-term storage.
Dangers: Rose hips seeds are covered in small hairs that can cause irritation to a person's throat if eaten.

Figure 75. Rose hips (Rosa spp.).
Found in Anna, Texas, on December 14th, 2019.

Figure 76. Rose hips (Rosa spp.).
Found in Anna, Texas, on December 14th, 2019.

Seaweed
Sargassum natans and Sargassum fluitans

Other Names: Sargassum
Range: East and Southeast Coast of Texas.
What to Use: Entire plant.
When to Find: Spring and summer.
Where to Find: Beaches.
How to Use: During the spring and summer, seaweed drifts will start to develop in the Gulf of Mexico and wash up on Texas beaches. All parts of the seaweed are edible, but it has a slightly bitter taste. The plant can be eaten raw, boiled or fried. It is best to collect the seaweed from the water and observe its color. Do not eat seaweed from contaminated water. It could be contaminated with a toxic algae (Vorderbruggen, Sargassum Seaweed, 2019).
Survival Uses: Seaweed can be eaten raw or cooked for short-term survival. It can be pickled for long-term storage.
Dangers: Possible contamination with toxic algae.

Figure 77. Seaweed (Sargassum spp.).
Found on Mustang Island State Park, May 7th, 2017.

Figure 78. Seaweed (Sargassum spp.).
Found on Mustang Island State Park, May 7th, 2017.

Stinging Nettle
Urtica spp.

Other Names: Common nettle, Nettle leaf, Nettle, Stinger.
Range: Most of Texas.
What to Use: Leaves and young stems.
When to Find: Summer and fall.
Where to Find: Shaded areas, woods, sunny fields, fence lines.
How to Use: Stinging Nettles are found worldwide and are one of the best survival foods. They are highly nutritious and contain assorted vitamins, minerals and protein. Stinging nettles have tiny microfilament hairs that contain formic acid. Formic acid is the same acid ants use to protect themselves, and anyone allergic to ants stings should avoid contact with this plant. The leaves and stems need to be crushed and boiled to remove the stinging hairs. Stinging nettle makes an excellent vitamin-rich tea (Boutenko, Wild Edibles, 2013).
Survival Uses: The leaves and young stems can be crushed and eaten raw for short-term survival or dried for long-term use. Stinging nettles have excellent fibers that can be processed from the mature stem for use as cordage.
Dangers: The leaves and stems contain tiny stinging hairs that contain formic acid and may result in severe anaphylactic shock.

Figure 79. Stinging nettle (Urtica spp.)
Found in Anna, Texas, on March 4th, 2017.

Figure 80. Stinging nettle (Urtica spp.)
Found in Anna, Texas, on March 4th, 2017.

Sunflower - Wild
Helianthus annuus

Other Names: Common Sunflower.
Range: Most of Texas.
What to Use: Young flowers and seeds.
When to Find: Summer and fall.
Where to Find: Sunny fields, ditches and fence lines.
How to Use: Wild Sunflower develop in the spring and will not die off until the first freeze. The flowers need to be harvested before they open and should be boiled to soften. The seeds will develop in early summer and are very small compared to commercial sunflower seeds. The seeds need to be harvest as soon as they develop to avoid competition from other animals (Vorderbruggen, Sunflower - Wild, 2019). The seeds are small enough to be eaten whole with the hull (Kane, 2017, 63).
Survival Uses: The seeds can be eaten raw for short-term survival. The young flower pods can be boiled and pickled for long-term storage. The sunflower stalk can be used as a straight spindle for a hand drill and/or small bow drill.
Dangers: None.

Figure 81. Sunflower (Helianthus annuus). Found in Live Oak, Texas, on June 15th, 2020.

Figure 82. Sunflower (Helianthus annuus). Found in Live Oak, Texas, on June 15th, 2020.

Thistle - Bull
Cirsium vulgare

Other Names: Spear Thistle, Common Thistle, Dodder, Boar Thistle.
Range: Most of Texas.
What to Use: All parts.
When to Find: Late winter to summer.
Where to Find: Fields, ditches and open areas.
How to Use: All types of thistles that grow in Texas are edible and are related to the Artichoke family. Bull Thistle grows tall and will have many sharp spines that cover the plant. The best way to harvest the plant is to cut the stem at the base and cut away the spiny leaves with a knife. Peel the outer layer off the stalk to get rid of the large fibers that cover it. The peeled stalk is used like celery and can be eaten raw or cooked. The stalks can also be pickled in vinegar to improve their taste. Bull Thistle is fibrous and makes excellent natural cordage (Boutenko, Wild Edibles, 2013).
Survival Uses: All parts of the plants can be eaten raw or cooked for short-term survival. All parts can be pickled for long-term storage.
Dangers: Thorns.

Figure 83. Bull Thistle (Cirsium vulgare).
Found in Anna, Texas, on February 5th, 2017.

Figure 84. Bull Thistle (Cirsium vulgare).
Found in Anna, Texas, on February 5th, 2017.

Thistle - Milk
Cirsium vulgare

Other Names: Blessed Milk Thistle, Marian Thistle, Saint Mary's Thistle, Mediterranean Milk Thistle, Variegated Thistle, Scotch Thistle, Cardus Marianus.
Range: Most of Texas.
What to Use: All parts.
When to Find: Late winter to summer.
Where to Find: Fields, ditches, open areas, and fence lines.
How to Use: Milk Thistle (Silybum marianum) can be even taller and more robust than Bull Thistle. The plant's size and the enormous violet flower make Milk Thistle easy to identify. The stems can be eaten after being peeled and can be pickled to improve the taste. The root can be roasted or dried and used as a coffee substitute. The seeds are used medicinally and can be dried whole or ground into flour for long-term storage (Vorderbruggen, Thistle - Milk, 2019).
Survival Uses: All parts of the plants can be eaten raw or cooked for short-term survival. All parts can be pickled for long-term storage.
Dangers: Do not confuse Milk Thistle with White Prickly Poppy (Argemone albiflora) (Vorderbruggen, Thistle - Milk, 2019).

Figure 85. Milk Thistle (Silybum marianum). Found in Anna, Texas, on February 5th, 2017.

Figure 86. Milk Thistle (Silybum marianum). Found in Anna, Texas, on April 7th, 2017.

Thistle - Sow
Sonchus oleraceus

Other Names: Common Sow Thistle, Smooth Sow Thistle, Annual Sow Thistle, Hare's Colwort, Hare's Thistle, Milky Tassel, Soft Thistle, Swinies.
Range: Most of Texas.
What to Use: All parts.
When to Find: Late winter to late fall.
Where to Find: Disturbed areas, yards, sidewalks, ditches and fields.
How to Use: Sow Thistle looks similar to a dandelion, and the entire plant is edible, but the root is very bitter. All parts of Sow Thistle are edible, but the stems and young leaves are the most palatable. The flower buds can be pickled and make a significant long-term source of food. The plant is highly nutritious and found throughout the majority of the year. The plant will disappear after the first freeze and start to regrow in late winter. Do not confuse Sow Thistle with the toxic Common Groundsel or Texas Groundsel (Vorderbruggen, Sow Thistle, 2019).
Survival Uses: All parts of the plants can be eaten raw or cooked for short-term survival. All parts can be pickled for long-term storage.
Dangers: Do not confuse Sow Thistle with the toxic Common Groundsel or Texas Groundsel.

Figure 87. Sow Thistle (Sonchus oleraceus).
Found in Anna, Texas, on February 17th, 2017.

Figure 88. Sow Thistle (Sonchus oleraceus).
Found in Anna, Texas, on February 22nd, 2017.

Wood Sorrel
Oxalis spp.

Other Names: Sourgrass, False Shamrocks, Common Yellow Oxalis, Yellow Wood Sorrel, Upright Yellow Wood Sorrel, Drummond's Wood-sorrel, Large-leaf Wood Sorrel, Pink Wood Sorrel, Strawberry Oxalis.
What to Use: All parts.
When to Find: All year.
Where to Find: Shady areas, yards, shady fields and fence rows.
How to Use: Wood Sorrel can be found worldwide and is an excellent plant for survival. The tubers can be eaten and taste similar to a radish but not as spicy. The seed pods and leaves are tangy due to the oxalic acid. Too much oxalic acid can lead to kidney stones. People who are prone to kidney stones should limit the amount of Wood Sorrel ingested. Boiling the plant will reduce the amount of oxalic acid and allow a person to eat more without the risk of developing kidney stones (Vorderbruggen, Wood Sorrel, 2019).
Survival Uses: Wood sorrel is found in most parts of the world. The entire plant is eaten raw or cooked for short-term survival and canned or pickled for long-term storage.
Dangers: Oxalic acid can lead to kidney stones.

Figure 89. Yellow Wood Sorrel (Oxalis dillenii).
Found in Live Oak, Texas, on February 23rd, 2017.

Figure 90. Pink Wood Sorrel (Oxalis crassipes).
Found in Live Oak, Texas, on February 23rd, 2017.

Yucca
Yucca spp.

Other Names: Aloe Yucca, Banana Yucca, Faxon Yucca, Torrey's Yucca, Spanish Dagger, Arkansas Yucca, Soapweed, San Angelo Yucca, Twist Leaf Yucca.
What to Use: Young flower stalks, flowers, and young seed pods.
When to Find: Spring and early summer.
Where to Find: Fields, brush land and hill country.
How to Use: There are more than 30 species of Yucca in Texas. The flower stalk is edible uncooked but tastes best when pickled. The flowers and edible fruits will develop in the spring season. The fruits need to be harvested soon after development before they become too hard. The seed pods can be roasted to make them more palatable (Kane 2017, 67-68).
Survival Uses: Yucca leaves contain some of the strongest natural fibers that can be found in Texas. The leaves can be quickly braided or reverse wrapped to make very strong cordage. The green or dried leaf fibers can also be used in a natural fire roll. The dried flower stalk makes one of the best spindles for hand drills and bow drill spindles due to the low ignition plant material. Native Americans would crush the roots and use the saponins to suffocate the fish in small ponds.
Dangers: Edible parts of the plant contain small amounts of saponins that may cause stomach upset.

Figure 91. Buckley yucca (Y. constricta).
Found in Live Oak, Texas, on February 8th, 2017.

Figure 92. Spanish dagger (Y. treculeana).
Found in Live Oak, Texas, on March 10th, 2017.

Edible Insects
Food

This chapter is designed to give the reader an estimate of nutrients for various common insects found in Texas, but it is not a comprehensive list. In most places around the world, insects are an essential part of the human diet. They are a good source of vital calories that can be hard to obtain from plant resources. Insects are high in macronutrients (e.g., protein, fats, and carbohydrates), essential for short-term and long-term survival. Macronutrients will vary even in the same species of insects. Insect levels of macronutrients depend on the area they live in and how much food is available. There are nine essential amino acids that humans can not create and have to come from a food source. It can be challenging to get the nine essential amino acids from plant sources. Insects that contain essential amino acids needed to prevent malnutrition are high in omega 3 and 6 fatty acids. Besides being rich in macronutrients, insects also contain vitamins and minerals. Many insects are rich in B vitamins, which are used in converting food to energy. Many are rich in iron and other minerals not found in most plants. By dry weight, 100 grams of both mealworms and crickets provide well over the daily requirements of Vitamins B2, B5, B7 and B9, with relatively high levels of Vitamins B1 and B3 (Finke, 2002).

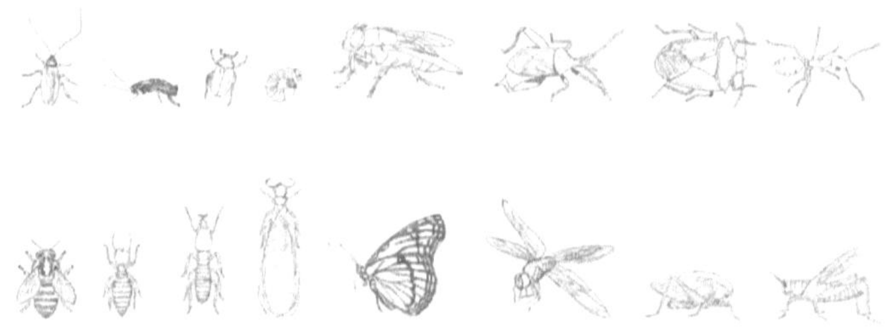

Figure 93. Edible Insects. This figure illustrates some of the common categories of edible insects.

Cockroaches (Blattodea)
Food

Cockroaches are often found under logs or in debris in the wild. They are typically located in moist, shady areas. Cockroaches can be caught by hand and are relatively easy to catch. They are packed with macronutrients, and due to their availability, they are commonly found during foraging. Cockroaches are 57.3 percent protein, 29.9 percent fat and 511 calories per 100-gram sample. The amount of nutrition makes cockroaches a valuable survival food, but they need to be adequately prepared before eating. (Rumpold & Schluter, 2013). Due to their propensity for scavenging, they tend to get into contaminated locations. They need to be cooked before eating to reduce the chance of bacterial related illness. Wings need to be removed before ingestion. Baking, frying, or roasting tend to be the best option for cockroaches. After cooking, they can be ground into flour to make them more palatable.

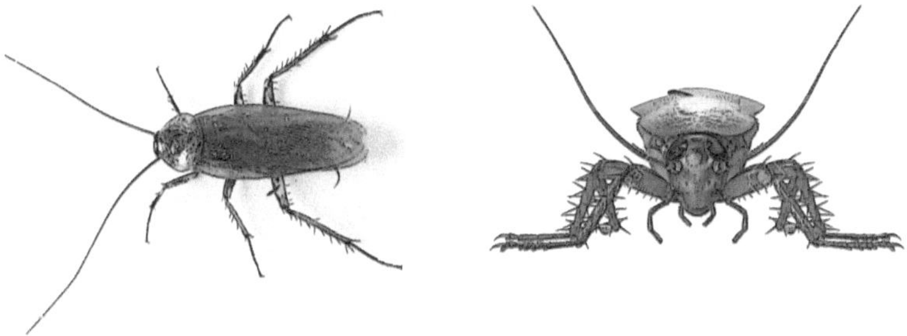

Figure 94. Cockroaches (Blattodea). This figure illustrates the top view and front view of a Cockroaches (Blattodea).

Beetles - Grubs (Coleoptera)
Food

Most beetles and grubs can be located in decaying logs or the ground. In Texas, June beetle grubs can be found in moist soil all through the year. Around the end of May and the early part of June, the beetles will immerge from the ground and can be found near bright objects at night. The beetles use the moon to navigate and fly towards any bright light, making it easy to harvest them at night. Rhinoceros beetle larvae are common in South Texas. The larvae are enormous compared to other beetle grubs and sometimes reach more than three inches in length and the diameter of a person's thumb. They are easily harvested by digging in compost, rotting plant material and soil. Beetles and grubs are 40.69 percent protein, 33.4 percent fat and 490 calories (Rumpold & Schluter, 2013).

Figure 95. Beetles and Grubs (Coleoptera). This figure illustrates the Rhinoceros beetles and grub (Coleoptera).

Flies (Diptera)
Food

Most flies are easy to harvest because they tend to find people in the wild. Depending on the location, it may be possible to find large quantities of flies. They tend to mass around large water bodies and decaying material, making it easy to collect them in large concentrations. In Texas, it may be challenging to find sufficient quantities of flies to make a substantial meal. Flies are high in protein but lower in fat than most insects. Flies contain 49.48 percent protein, 22.75 percent fat and 409.78 calories per 100- gram sample (Rumpold & Schluter, 2013).

Figure 96. Flies (Diptera). This figure illustrates and provides examples of Flies (Diptera).

True Bugs (Hemiptera)
Food

True bugs are a broad classification of many types of bugs that consists of cicadas, aphids, assassin bugs and many others. True Bugs (Hemiptera) can be found under logs or on plants. They are easy to catch but hard to collect in large quantities. Cicadas are common throughout the summer months in Texas. Many types of aphids are small and difficult to gather in mass. Some assassin bugs are carriers of Chagas and need to be collected with care. They contain 48.33 percent protein, 30.26 fat and 478.99 calories per 100-gram sample (Rumpold & Schluter, 2013).

Figure 97. True Bugs (Hemiptera). This figure illustrates and provides examples of True Bugs (Hemiptera).

Ants and Bees (Hymenoptera)
Food

Ants and bees are excellent survival food. They can be collected in large quantities and without a lot of caloric expenditure. Bees are unique to other insects because they also produce honey. It is often best to leave the bees alive and try to harvest the honey. It can be dangerous to harvest in Texas due to the Africanized colonies that take over the European hives. Smoke can be used to soothe European bees but should not be attempted with killer bees. Honey provides a calorically dense food and has antiseptic properties. Ants and bees provide 46.47 percent protein, 25.09 percent fat and 484.45 calories per 100-gram sample (Rumpold & Schluter, 2013).

Figure 98. Ants and Bees (Hymenoptera). This figure illustrates and provides examples of Ants and Bees (Hymenoptera).

Termites (Isoptera)
Food

Termites are a great survival food, and they are easy to collect in other parts of the world. In Texas, they can be found in decaying logs and debris. The species of termite native to Texas are small but can be found in large quantities. They are not as easy to collect in mass as other termites outside Texas. Some primates like Chimpanzees harvest termite by using tools. Termites consist of almost equal amounts of fats and protein. They use a small twig that termites climb, and then the chimp uses their lips to extract the termites from the twig. They are a common food source in some countries. Termites contain 35.34 percent protein, 32.74 percent fat and 469.8 calories per 100-gram sample (Rumpold & Schluter, 2013).

Figure 99. Termites (Isoptera). This figure illustrates and provides examples of Termites (Isoptera).

Butterflies and Moths (Lepidoptera)
Food

Butterflies and moths are not the best survival food due to the difficulty to capture enough of the insect to make a meal. Many butterflies and moths are poisonous (e.g., Monarch and Pipevine Swallowtail) and need to be avoided. "Only a few moths, butterflies, and caterpillars (order Lepidoptera) are edible. These include the maguey worm, silkworm, mopane worm, and bamboo worm" (Helmenstine, 2021). No single butterfly or moth is poisonous enough to kill a human, but it is essential to know the type of butterfly or moth before ingestion. Butterflies and moths contain 45.38 percent protein, 27.66 percent fat and 508.89 calories per 100-gram sample (Rumpold & Schluter, 2013).

Figure 100. Butterflies and Moths (Lepidoptera). This figure illustrates and provides examples of Butterflies and Moths (Lepidoptera).

Dragonflies and Damselflies
(Odonata) Food

Dragonflies and damselflies can be found in large quantities near large bodies of water, rivers and streams. It may be necessary to use a net to capture them in flight. It can be challenging to capture them while they are stationary due to their wide range of vision. In Texas, they can be found in large quantities during the Fall. Dragonflies and damselflies are high in protein but lower in fat. They contain 55.23 percent protein, 19.83 percent fat and 431.33 calories per 100-gram sample (Rumpold & Schluter, 2013).

Figure 101. Dragonflies and Damselflies (Odonata). This figure illustrates and provides examples of Dragonflies and Damselflies (Odonata).

Crickets and Grasshoppers
(Orthoptera) Food

Crickets and Grasshoppers (Orthoptera) are among the best survival foods due to their availability and ease of capture. Crickets are easily located under logs or debris. Grasshoppers can be found in large quantities during the summer. Locusts will sometimes swarm in Texas and can be one of the most significant food sources due to the pest's quantity. In some countries, some people resort to eating locust when the pest eats their crops. It is ironic that the farmers still harvest a nutritious meal that is often more calorically dense than the foods they would have harvested. Crickets are currently being used as a protein supplement in some foods. Crickets, grasshoppers and locusts are 61.32 percent protein, 13.41 percent fat and 426.25 calories per 100-gram sample (Rumpold & Schluter, 2013).

Figure 102. Crickets and Grasshoppers (Orthoptera). This figure illustrates and provides examples of Crickets and Grasshoppers (Orthoptera).

Cordage, Knots and Hitches
Primitive Engineering Essentials

Understanding how to make cordage from natural resources and tie knots is an essential skill for primitive engineering. Making cordage allows a person to make a rope to secure objects, build shelter make baskets, and other essential engineer projects needed to survive. Braiding can be used to make natural cordage quickly. Reverse wrapping fibers is more time consuming but allows for the production of stronger cordage. Knots and hitches are required to bind objects together (e.g., shelter building, climbing, raft construction, etc.) This chapter will describe the most common methods to make and use cordage for primitive engineering projects.

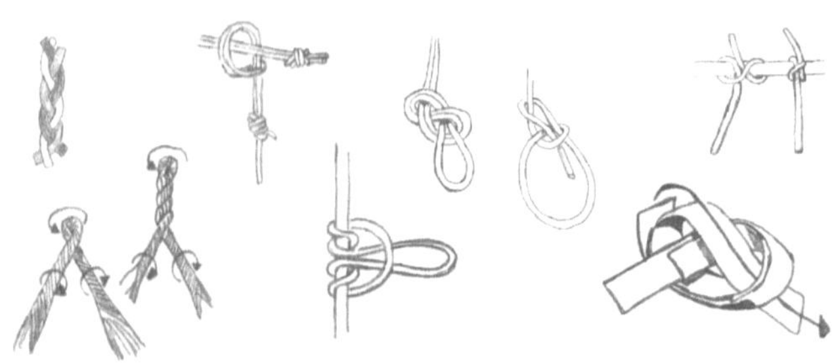

Figure 103. Cordage, Knots and Hitches. This figure illustrates and provides examples of Cordage, Knots and Hitches.

Reverse Wrap Cordage
Primitive Engineering Essentials

The reverse wrap is one of the best methods to add strength to natural fibers to make cordage. Yucca and agave have some of the best natural fibers to make natural cordage. The reverse wrap method is used for applications requiring strong cordage with flexibility and tensile strength (e.g., shelter, rafts, and bow drill string). The process of making reverse wrapped cordage is time-consuming. It consists of twisting the fibers tightly until they form a loop in the line. The process starts by pinching the loop and twist each line clockwise. Both strands are twisted around each other in a counterclockwise position. The splices must be at least two to three inches apart.

Figure 104. Reverse Wrap Cordage. This figure illustrates and provides examples of Reverse Wrap Cordage.

Braiding Cordage
Primitive Engineering Essentials

Braiding is one of the fastest methods to turn natural fibers into useful cordage. Yucca and agave have some of the best natural fibers to make natural cordage. Braiding is used for applications when cordage is needed fast or reverse wrapped cordage into stronger cordage. The three-strand braid is one of the simplest and easiest methods of braining. It consists of three separate stands being braided together to increase tensile strength. The outside strands repeatedly alternate over the center strand. For example, the left stand crosses the center stand and become the new center. Then the right crosses the new center strand and become the new center. The process continues until the need for a splice. All splices need to be at least 2-3 inches apart. If splices are too close together, they reduce the tensile strength of the cordage.

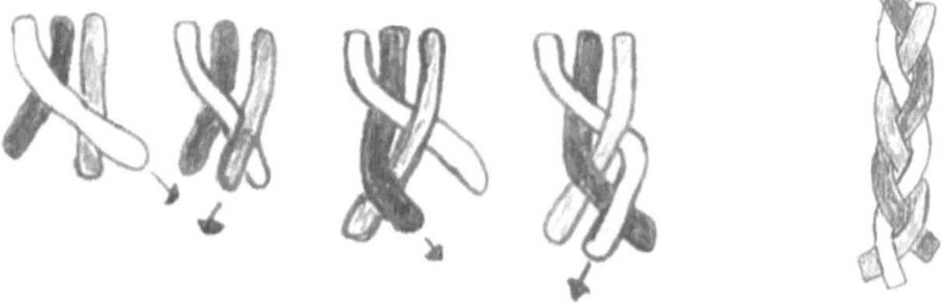

Figure 105. Braiding Cordage. This figure illustrates and provides examples of braiding cordage.

Clove Hitch
Primitive Engineering Essentials

The clove hitch consists of two half hitches and is often is used to bind two limbs together. The strength of the hitch is the ability to adjust the tension without completely untieing the knot. The clove hitch may be easily adjusted, but that is also its weakness. It should not be used on a moving object or for applications requiring a secure knot for safety (e.g., climbing). The primary use for the clove hitch during primitive survival situations is for shelter and raft construction. It can also be used to secure cordage to a thumb loop or gas pedal hand drill. If the clove hitch is used for movement applications, more half-hitches will be necessary to prevent the hitch from loosening.

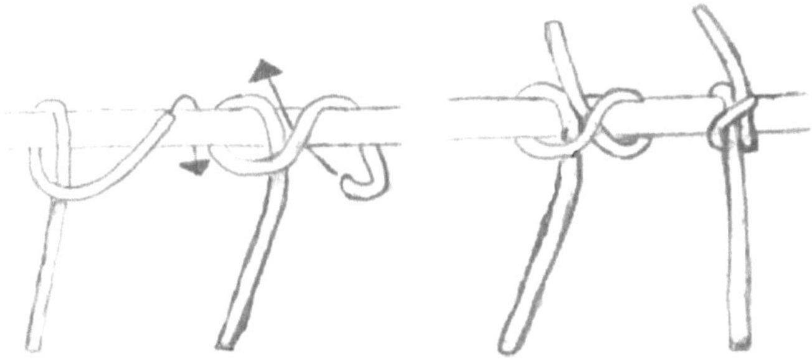

Figure 106. Clove Hitch. This figure illustrates and provides examples of a clove hitch.

Round Turn & Two Half Hitches
Primitive Engineering Essentials

The Round Turn plus Two Half Hitches is similar to the Clove Hitch. The hitch is used to secure a line to an object. The main advantage it the hitch can be easily untied after a load has been placed on it. It should not be used for applications that require a secure knot (e.g., climbing, transporting a load, etc.) because it can be shaken loose. One of the primary applications is to suspend an object to another object. For example, the hitch can hang food in a tree to prevent animals from getting into a container or suspending a container from a tripod above a fire. The round turn plus half hitches allow the object to be removed without struggling to untie a knot.

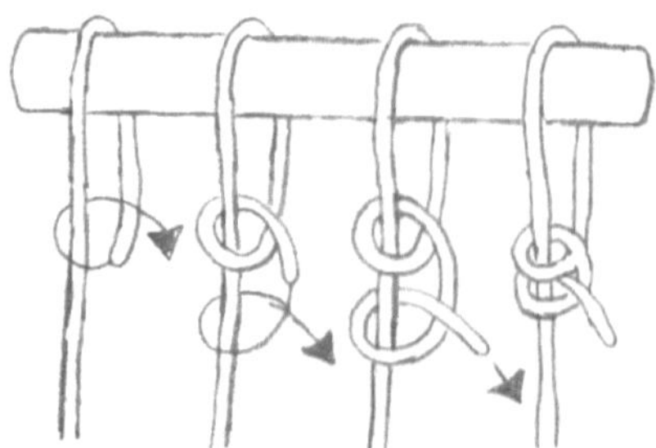

Figure 107. Round Turn & Two Half Hitches. This figure illustrates and provides examples of a Round Turn & Two Half Hitches.

Square Knot
Primitive Engineering Essentials

The square knot is a binding knot used to secure two ends of a line. Both sections of cordage must be equal in size. The knot has multiple applications and is useful when a fast and easy connection is needed. For example, if another line is tied to a limb, the square knot is used to secure another line. The square knot's most common applications are to secure a boat to the line, elevate food off the ground, and suspend a container when boiling water with a tripod. The process to tie a square knot involves taking the end of each rope in different hands—the right-hand moves over and under the rope in the left hand. Take the end of the rope in the left hand over and under the one now in the right. Dress the knot by pulling both running ends at the same time (BoyScoutsofAmerica, 2021).

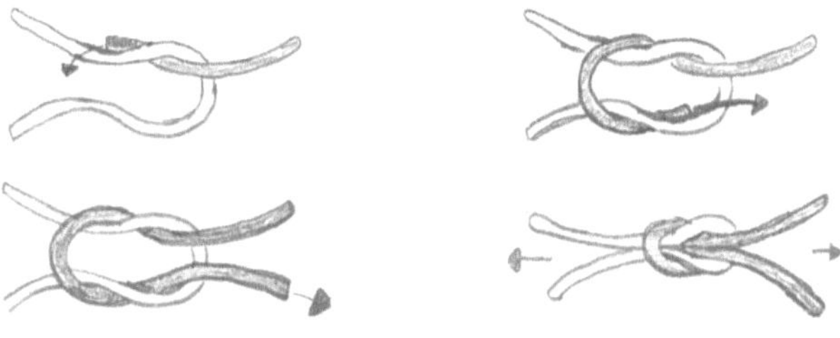

Figure 108. Square Knot. This figure illustrates and provides examples of the square knot.

Sheet Bend
Primitive Engineering Essentials

The sheet bend is similar to the square knot but involves binding two different sized ropes. Both sections of cordage are not equal in size, and the technique prevents the knot from slipping. The knot has similar applications to the square knot and is useful when a fast and easy connection is needed. It can be easily untied once a load has been placed on it. The sheet bend's most common applications are to secure a boat to the line, elevate food off the ground, and suspend a container when boiling water with a tripod. The process to tie a sheet bend is similar to the square knot with the edition of crossing the smaller line's end under itself inside the loop.

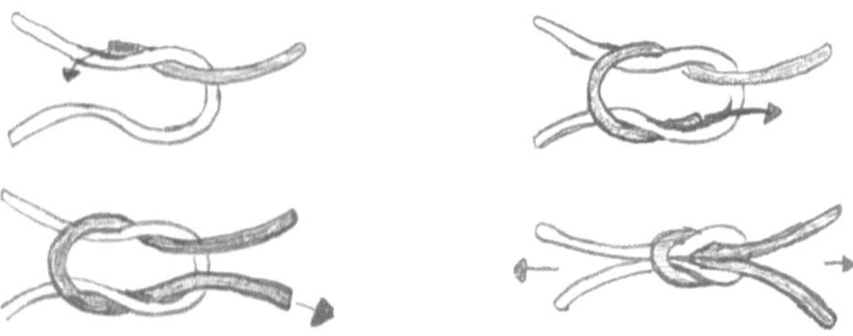

Figure 109. Sheet Bend. This figure illustrates and provides examples of the sheet bend.

Lark's Head
Primitive Engineering Essentials

The lark's head also referred to as a cow hitch, quickly attaches one line to another rope. The knot can be easily untied after a load has been placed on it. Use of the lark's head is not as dependent on the size of the two types of cordage. As the load on the line increases, so does the tightness of the knot. Tieing the lark's head requires a loop in one line and an overhand knot in the other. The overhand knot is required to prevent the loop from slipping off the line when tension increases. The lark's head is one of the quickest and fastest methods to connect and disconnect two ropes as long as tension in the line can be easily reduced.

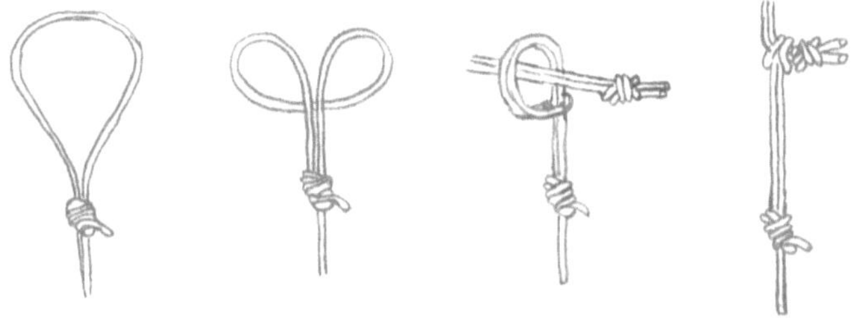

Figure 110. Lark's Head. This figure illustrates and provides examples of the lark's head.

Double Figure Eight
Primitive Engineering Essentials

The double figure-eight knot(e.g., figure-eight on a bight, figure-eight follow-through, Flemish loop, or Flemish eight) is excellent for creating a fixed loop at the end of a rope (101knots.com, 2021). It is easy to untie after a load has been placed on it. It is one of the main knots used in climbing. Fixed loops can be used in various applications ranging from climbing, boating, and tying other knots. The knot is secure and is one of the safest knots to use when safety is a priority. It is also simple to tie and easy to learn. It is often one of the first knots a person will learn when involved in climbing.

Figure 111. Double Figure Eight. This figure illustrates and provides examples of a double figure-eight knot.

Bowline
Primitive Engineering Essentials

The bowline knot is a standard method to create a fixed loop at the end of a rope. It is easy to untie after it has been tensioned with resistance. It is one of the main knots used in climbing. Fixed loops can be used in various applications ranging from climbing, boating, and tying other knots. This variation of the bowline knot is not secure enough for climbing. There are modifications to the bowline that can be used for climbing applications. The standard bowline is simple to tie and easy to learn. It is often one of the first knots a person will learn when involved in boating and scouting.

Figure 112. Bowline. This figure illustrates and provides examples of the bowline knot.

Poacher's and Fisherman's Knot
Primitive Engineering Essentials

The Poacher's knot is to create an adjustable loop at the end of a rope. It is easy to untie after it has been tensioned with resistance. It is similar to a Fisherman's knot with one fewer wrap around the rope. Both knots are commonly used in hunting and fishing. An adjustable loop allows the diameter to be reduced to catch animals for trapping or when attaching a hook to a fishing line. Both knots should not be used for climbing or other applications requiring a level of safety. The Poacher's and Fisherman's knot are simple to tie and easy to learn. It is often one of the first knots a person will learn when involved in fishing and trapping.

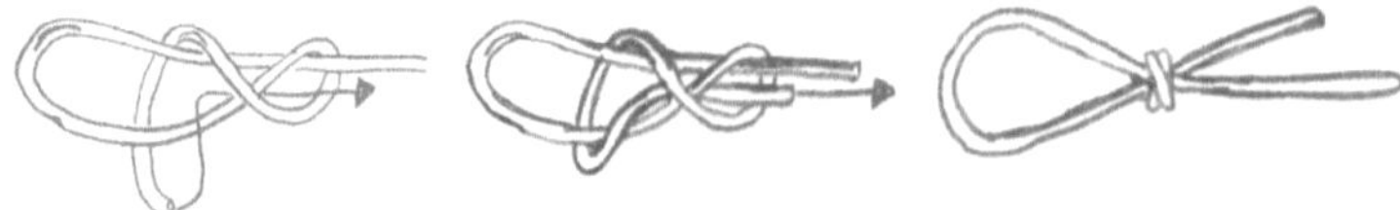

Figure 113. Poacher's Knot. This figure illustrates and provides examples of the Poacher's knot.

Overhand Knot
Primitive Engineering Essentials

The Overhand knot (e.g., knot and half knot) is one of the most common knots and is often the first to learn for most daily activities. The knot is used as the primary stages of other knots and is used to form when tieing the overhand loop knot, Fisherman's knot, square knot (101knots.com, 2021). If the figure-eight follow-through is tied wrong in the beginning stage, it will form an overhand knot. It can be difficult to untie after it has been tensioned with resistance. It can tie off newly made cordage and be used as a stopper knot when sewing in survival situations. The knot can be used to hold stands of cordage together when braiding.

Figure 114. Overhand Knot. This figure illustrates and provides examples of the overhand knot.

Prusik Knot
Primitive Engineering Essentials

The Prusik Knot is named after Austrian mountaineer Karl Prusik (101knots.com, 2021). The knot is a type of friction hitch that is attached to another rope or pole. It is a unidirectional hitch and can be used to ascend a line or any cylinder-shaped object with a uniform shape. One of the primary applications in survival is ascending a line or making a bow drill. The Prusik Knot bow drill allows for a straight stick to be used as a bow when making a fire. A straight stick is often easier to find than a bent one of suitable length. The use of the Prusik Knot allows for additional friction and prevents the spindle from slipping. The technique allows for a more efficient application of the skill, requiring less effort to make a fire. The straight stick also acts as a guide allowing a beginner an easier time learning the skill.

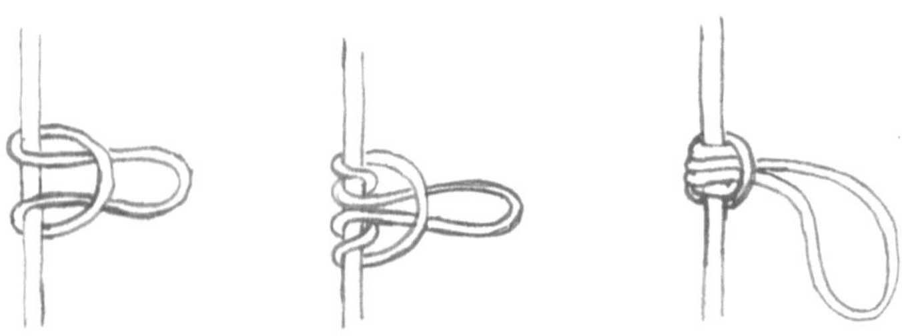

Figure 115. Prusik Knot. This figure illustrates and provides examples of the Prusik Knot.

Water Knot
Primitive Engineering Essentials

The Water Knot (e.g., ring bend, grass knot, tape knot) essentially uses two overhand knots and one strand of webbing that follows through the first (101knots.com, 2021). The knot is best used to secure two ends of webbing. Unlike the Fisherman's knot, the loop will not be adjustable. The Water Knot is the best technique when a fixed loop is needed when tieing two webbing (e.g., flat strap) ends together. The knot is best for flat materials such as tape, leather and straps. The Water Knot should not be used for tieing two pieced of rope together due to the risk of slipping and coming untied. The most common applications are climbing anchors, shelter design, raft building and other construction applications involving webbing.

Figure 116. Water Knot. This figure illustrates and provides examples of the water knot.

Munter Hitch
Primitive Engineering Essentials

The Munter Hitch is "named after a Swiss mountain guide, Werner Munter, who played an important role in popularizing it with mountaineers around 1970" (101knots.com, 2021). The knot is commonly used to belay or repel in climbing but lower a heavy object in survival situations. The Munter is commonly used in conjunction with a carabiner but can be used around poles, pipes or another cylindrical object. One of the main application to survival situations is to control a heavy object when lowering it to another location (e.g., shelter building, raft lowering, and wilderness first aid). If a person is injured, the Munter Hitch can be sued to slow a person's descent down a hillside when attempting to move a victim to safety.

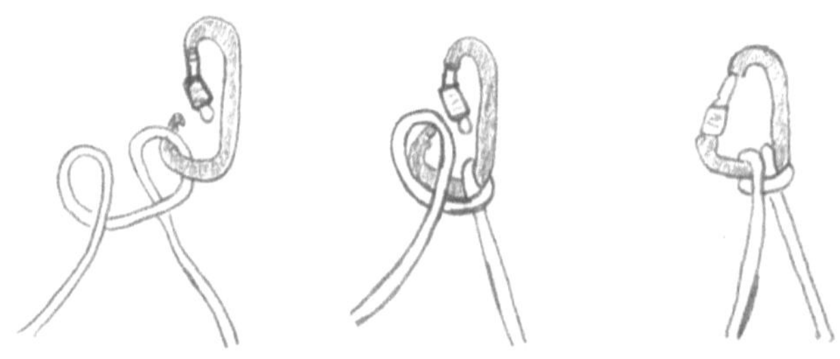

Figure 117. Munter Hitch. This figure illustrates and provides examples of the Munter Hitch.

Hunting, Trapping and Fishing
Food

Hunting, trapping and fishing are some of the best methods to collect calorically dense food. Animals provide large amounts of calories and other primitive resources that can be used in survival situations. Large game animals are rich in protein and fats, but their hide can be tanned for a range of other uses (e.g., shelter, clothing, bowstring, containers, etc.). Traditional hunting methods (e.g., active hunting) are statistically unreliable and, depending on the method, can result in significant caloric expenditure. Traps, snares and weirs (e.g., passive hunting) are an excellent way to hunt without spending too much energy. As more traps and snares are set up, the statistical chance of catching an animal increases. The best time to create the material needed to construct traps and snares is at night while sitting around the fire or inside a shelter. Making traps and snares allows a person to occupy their mind at night and save calories by passively hunting. Efficient use of time can help preserve mental and physical energy.

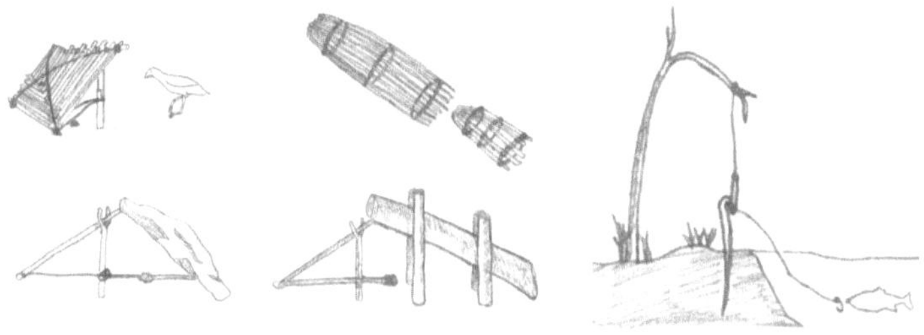

Figure 118. Traps, Snares and Weirs. This figure illustrates and provides examples of the traps, snares and weirs.

Figure Four Deadfall
Hunting, Trapping and Fishing

Figure Four Deadfalls are one of the most common primitive trapping methods used in a survival situation. It requires no cordage and is easy to construct. Using a wedge or "Y" stick for the central support prevents the trap from yawing. Yawing can lead to the trap fall to the side and is difficult to set up. It may be necessary to use stakes on each side of the weight to prevent yawing. The stakes also make the deadfall more efficient at trapping animals. They limit the avenues of escape and force the animal to exit the way they entered into the trap. The stakes result in delaying the animal's escape and increases the likelihood that the deadfall will crush them.

Strengths: Figure Four Deadfalls are simple to create and set up. They can be quick to create, which allows for multiple to be made at one time.

Weakness: Deadfalls crush the animal and may result in contamination from ruptured internal organs.

Materials: Almost any straight sticks can be used to create the trap.

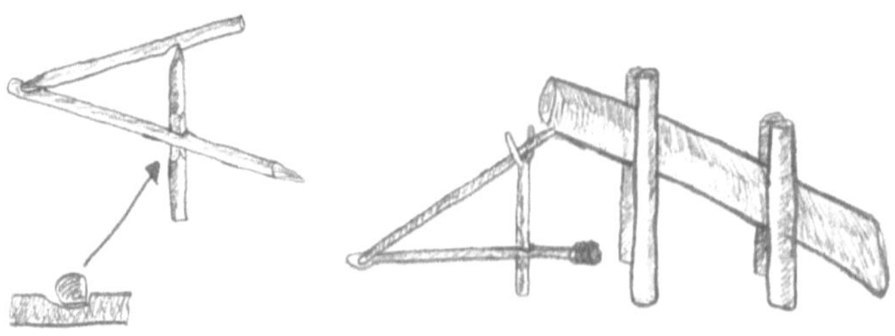

Figure 119. Figure Four Deadfall. This figure illustrates and provides examples of the Figure Four Deadfall.

Paiute Deadfall
Hunting, Trapping and Fishing

The Paiute Deadfall is a primitive trap that has a similar design to the Figure Four Deadfall. The design "is named after the native Paiute peoples – nomadic hunters and gatherers who depended on wild plants and animals" (Homesteadtelegraph, 2021). The weight-bearing stick that supports the weight is secured to the trigger stick by cordage. The central support stick can be a "Y" stick or utilize the same notch design as the Figure Four application. The bait stick is wedged against the weight used for the deadfall. The bait should cover the bait stick, so the animal has to pull on it. The difficulty of removing the bait will make it more likely the animal will trigger the trap. This Paiute design is easier to set up and is relies on cordage.

Strengths: The Piaute design is easier to set up than the Figure Four Deadfall. As long as cordage is available, many traps can be made and set up in very little time.

Weakness: The Piaute trap requires cordage. Deadfalls crush the animal and may result in contamination from ruptured internal organs. The trap needs to be checked often to reduce the risk of tainted meat.

Materials: Almost any straight sticks can be used to create the trap. Cordage may need to be created from natural fibers.

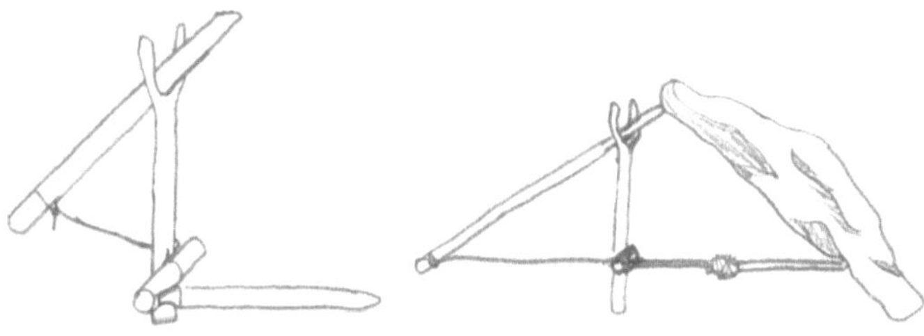

Figure 120. Paiute Deadfall. This figure illustrates and provides examples of the Paiute Deadfall.

Trigger Snare
Hunting, Trapping and Fishing

A trigger snare has various application to active and passive hunting. The snare is used actively by herding animals towards the locations where snares are set up. Teams of people make noise which scares the animals towards the locations where the traps are set up. Actively hunting with snares is often used in conjunction with other forms of trapping (e.g., pits, trigger spears, etc.) The trigger snare works by locking two branches together. Limbs are cut from the branch to form a trigger. A flexible limb is used to act as the spring to tension the noose around the animal's body part when the trigger is set off. It is essential to place the noose along an existing trail and the bait on both sides of the noose. No matter the travel direction, the animal will need to walk through to get the bait. If the trigger snare is used for fishing, the tension will set the hook. It is essential the fish is not pulled out of the water, or it may escape.

Strengths: The triggering mechanism is easy and quick to create. Several traps can be set up quickly depending on the available materials.

Weakness: The trap requires cordage, flexible limbs and should be set up on an existing game trail for passive hunting.

Materials: The trap requires cordage and flexible limbs that are strong enough to set the noose.

Figure 121. Trigger Snare. This figure illustrates and provides examples of the Trigger Snare.

Fishing Weir
Hunting, Trapping and Fishing

A fishing weir is one of the simplest and easiest methods to trap and catch fish. The weir can be used actively and passively to capture fish. There are several designs, but this chapter will focus on the "M" design. Sticks are broken and driven into a shallow area near a bank and formed into an "M" shape. The opening is located in the middle of the M so fish can enter. Bait is placed in the center of the weir to attract the fish. Once the fish have eaten the bait, they have a difficult time trying to find the exit. Debris is placed along the M's inner portion to give the fish a place to hide. Before entering the weir, it is necessary to close the entrance to prevent the fish from escaping. Once the escape route has been closed, the fish can be easily caught by hand or with a net.

Strengths: Weirs are easy to create and can be used for active and passive hunting.

Weakness: The trap requires shallow water that a person can easily wade through.

Materials: Small rocks or sticks are needed to form the parameter of the weir. Debris is needed to give the fish a place to hide.

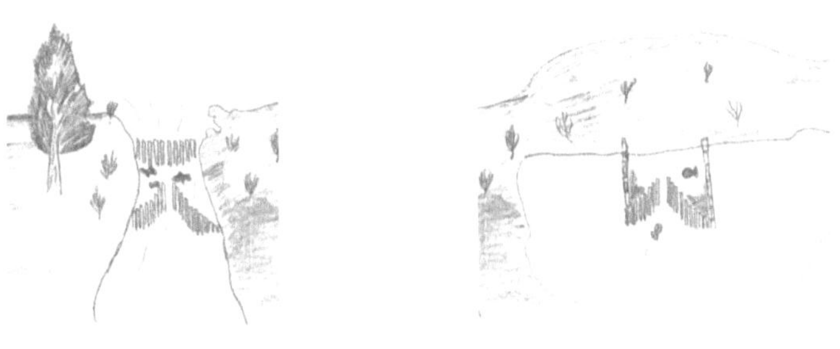

Figure 122. Fishing Weir. This figure illustrates and provides a diagram of a fishing weir.

Arapuca Bird Trap
Hunting, Trapping and Fishing

"An arapuca or aripuca is a handcrafted trap used by the Guaraní to catch birds, monkeys and other small animals" (en.wikipedia.org, 2021). The trap is easy to make, but it requires cordage. The sticks that form the frame of the trap are cut and stacked in a pyramid-shape. Cordage is attached at the base and crosses the top of the trap in an X pattern. The lines are tightened to compress and hold the frame together. The sticks that form the frame need to be equal in size and small enough to prevent the animal from escaping. The top sticks can be pulled out to allow the animal to be removed after being trapped. The trap's opening needs to be just large enough for a person's hand to fit inside to limit the animal from escaping. The traditional trigger was a split stick design, but a Paiute or Figure Four Deadfall can also be used as a trigger.

Strengths: Arapuca Bird Traps are easy to create and can be used for passive hunting.

Weakness: The trap requires straight sticks that form the frame, and they may be challenging to locate in some environments.

Materials: The materials required are straight sticks of almost equal size and cordage.

Figure 123. Arapuca Bird Trap. This figure illustrates and provides a diagram of an Arapuca Bird Trap.

Straight Stick Fish Trap
Hunting, Trapping and Fishing

The straight stick fish trap is easy to make, but it requires cordage. The sticks that form the frame need to be straight and relatively equal in size. Cordage secures the frame to at least three concentric circles. Freshly cut green limbs are used to form the circle. It may be necessary to steam, boil or heat the green limbs to increase their flexibility depending on the size and type of wood used. The spacing between the straight sticks needs to be small enough to prevent the fish from escaping. Vines can be woven in the spaces between the frame decrease the chance of fish escaping. It is easier to find resources to build a straight stick fish trap compared to other woven methods. It is easier to build and takes less time. The trap consists of two funnel-shaped parts. The smaller funnel should fit inside the more extensive and have an opening at the end to allow fish to enter the trap.

Strengths: Straight Stick FishTraps are easy to create and can be used for passive hunting. The resources are easier to find than other methods and take little time to assemble.

Weakness: The trap requires straight sticks that form the frame, and they may be challenging to locate in some environments.

Materials: The materials required are straight sticks of almost equal size, flexible limbs to form the circles and cordage.

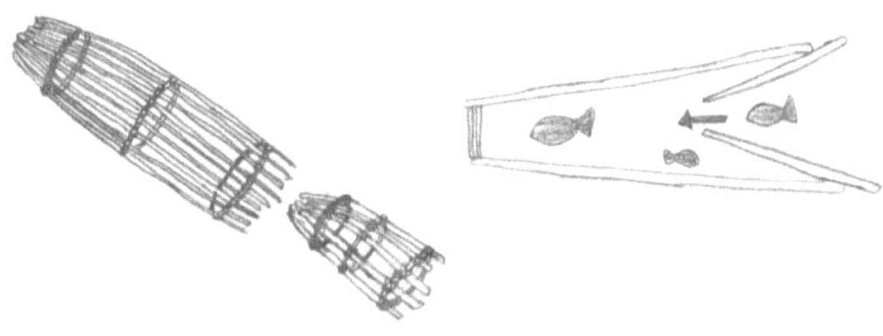

Figure 124. Straight Stick Fish Traps. This figure illustrates and provides a diagram of the Straight Stick Fish Trap.

Primitive Navigation
Primitive Navigation and Self Rescue

It is unwise to be dependant on modern technology for navigation. Few people are prepared when lost in nature and often do not have access to working equipment. Even if the modern equipment works, many types are dependent on a signal. Many areas worldwide do not have the infrastructure to support modern technology, and modern technology is also dependant on energy storage. Batteries have limited power and are influenced by the environment. Battery storage can be affected by cold, heat, water and other elements of nature. Primitive navigation is a core component when learning survival skill. It should be the foundation of all people involved in outdoor activities. It allows a person to self-rescue and can prevent a survival situation from becoming worse.

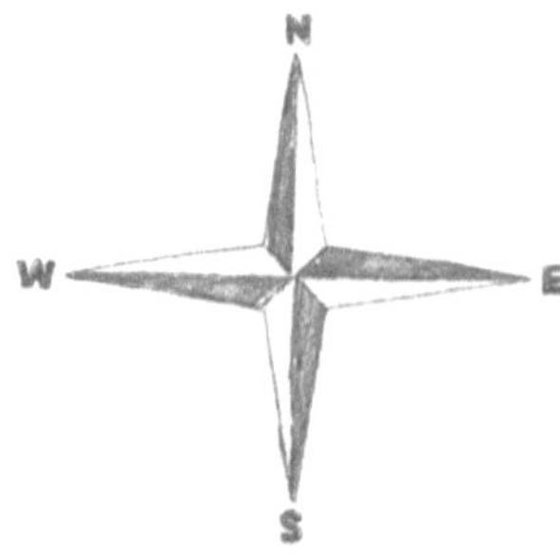

Figure 125. Primitive Navigation. This figure illustrates and provides a diagram of elements of primitive navigation.

Never Eat Sour Watermelon
Primitive Navigation and Self Rescue

The first step when attempting to navigate is to find the direction of travel. The first step is to find one general direction. Celestial objects, magnetism or shadows of the sun and moon can be used to find a general direction. If one direction is known, the Never Eat Sour Watermelon mnemonic can find all other directions. For example, if a person knows north, they can move ninety degrees clockwise from north to find east. Ninety degrees clockwise from the east direction is south, and ninety degrees from the south is west. The most common celestial objects used to find a general direction are Polaris (e.g., North Star in the Northern Hemisphere), the crescent moon (e.g., South in the northern latitudes), sun and moon rise and setting (e.g., East and West). Some celestial navigation is more accurate than others. All rely on a full or partial view of the sky. Other methods of primitive navigation are dependant on the availability of natural resources (e.g., iron and straight sticks). Still, they can be used in conjunction with the mnemonic Never Eat Sour Watermelon. The mnemonic is essential to allow a person to navigate and increase the likelihood of self-rescue.

Strengths: The mnemonic relies on methods of finding at least one direction.

Weakness: The mnemonic relies on other methods of finding at least one general direction, and some techniques do not allow for an exact direction.

Materials: Some techniques like sun and moon dials require objects that cast a shadow (e.g., sticks, trees, rocks).

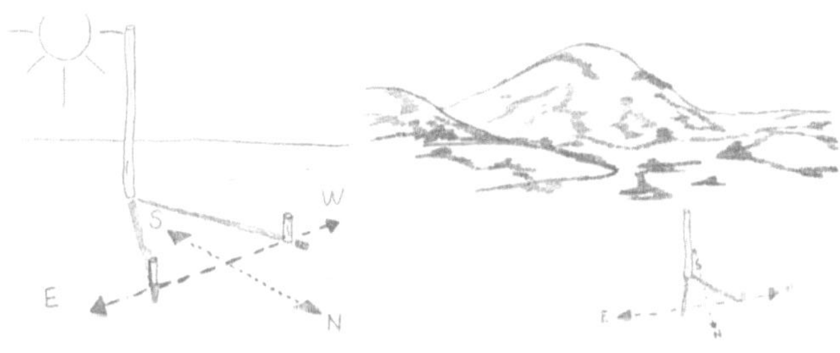

Figure 126. Never Eat Sour Watermelon. This figure illustrates and provides a diagram of the Never Eat Sour Watermelon mnemonic.

Sundial Navigation
Primitive Navigation and Self Rescue

This form of primitive navigation relies on a clear or partially clear sky. The surface must be flat to prevent distortion of the shadow and improve accuracy. Place a stick (e.g., dial) three foot in length into the ground and mark the shadow with an object. Wait fifteen minutes and mark the new location of the shadow. Continue this process until the shadow shortens and lengthens. The sundial's shadow is affected by latitude, and the East to West line will not be exact during the majority of the year but can be used as a rough estimate of the general directions. This method works best when finding an estimate of North and must be done near solar noon. Solar noon is defined by the Sun at the "highest point in the sky and can be observed using a sundial" using a straight stick (Quaschning, 2021). When a shadow is tracked throughout the day, the shortest part shadow will indicate solar noon and indicate an estimate of North. The general direction of North can be used in conjunction with the Never Eat Sour Watermelon mnemonic to find the other general directions.

Strengths: This sundial application is reliable when finding North.
Weakness: This method is less reliable when attempted early in the morning or late in the evening.
Materials: This method requires straight objects three to four feet in length to cast a shadow on a flat surface.

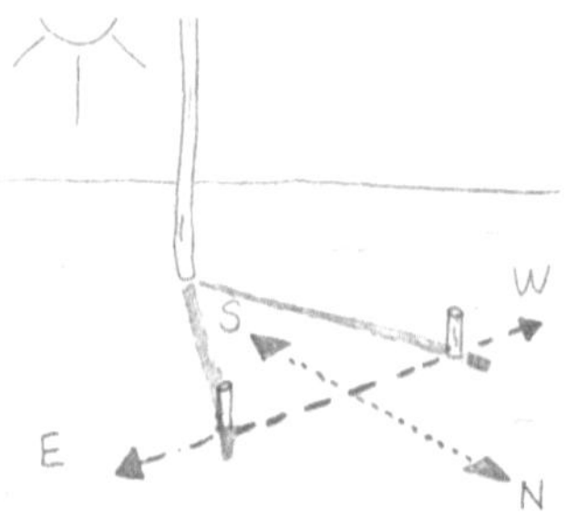

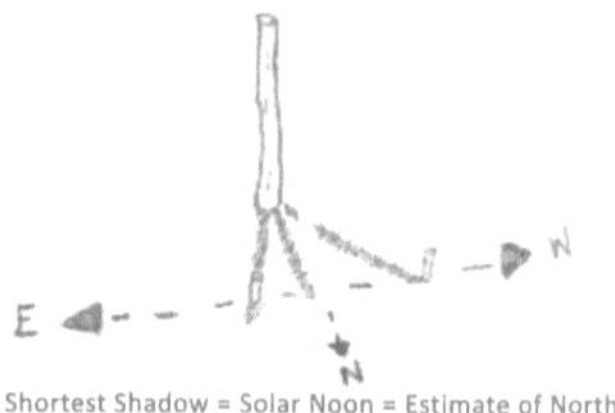

Figure 127. Sundial Navigation. This figure illustrates and provides a diagram of using a straight stick as a sundial to find North.

Night Navigation
Primitive Navigation and Self Rescue

Night navigation requires an unobstructed or partially unobstructed view of the night sky. The most common method in the Northern Hemisphere is to find a reliable general direction is the North Star (e.g., Polaris). The easiest way to find the North Star is to locate the Big Dipper, located in the Ursa Major constellation. The first step involves finding the two brightest stars that make up the edge of the Big Dippers scoop and drawing a line up towards the tail of the Little Dipper"s (e.g., Ursa Minor). The North Star is located in the Little Dippers tail. Another less accurate method of nighttime celestial navigation is to use the moon. The easiest but less accurate method involves drawing a line from a crescent moon's points towards the horizon. "The line that joins the points of a crescent moon together is at right-angles to this east and west line (Naturalnavigator.com, 2021). This technique will also point in the general direction of the south but is not exact. The moon can also provide an estimate of east and west based on its position to the sun. "Since the moon reflects the sun's light, its bright side will be pointing to the direction of the sun, approximately east or west" (Naturalnavigator.com, 2021). All methods mentioned above are used in conjunction with the mnemonic Never Eat Sour Watermelon to find all other general directions.
Strengths: Using the North Star is a reliable method of night navigation.
Weakness: All methods rely on an unobstructed view of the night sky.
Materials: No materials are required.

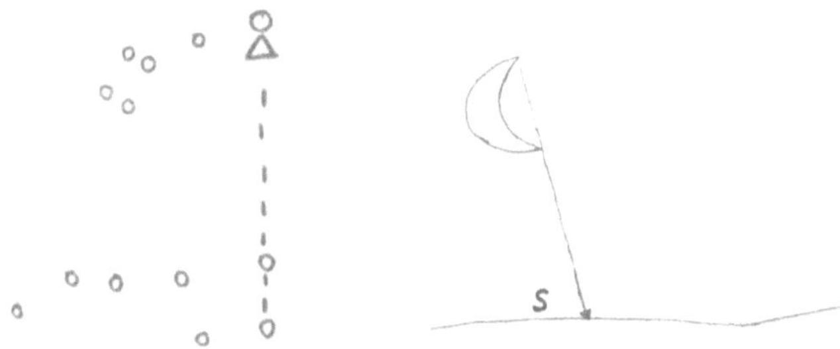

Figure 128. Night Navigation. This figure illustrates and provides a diagram of the two most common techniques that can be used quickly to navigate at night.

Visual Bearings
Primitive Navigation and Self Rescue

Once a direction has been determined, a visual bearing can help a person stay in their intended travel direction. A visual bearing can be a distinct point on the horizon (e.g., mountain range, tree, etc.). In open terrain, it is necessary to find a point as far away as possible in the direction of travel. The further away the object is, the easier it will be to follow a straight line. Large, easily identifiable objects that stand out require fewer corrections as the person navigates in the direction of travel. If a person is in a location where a line of sight is narrow, such as a forest, it may be necessary to blaze a tree or use breadcrumbing to keep travel direction until the visual bearing marker can be seen.

Strengths: Visual bearings are one of the best methods to follow the direction of travel.
Weakness: Visual bearing requires a periodic line of sight to verify a person is travelling in the intended direction of travel.
Materials: A visual bearing requires a large, easily identifiable distant object.

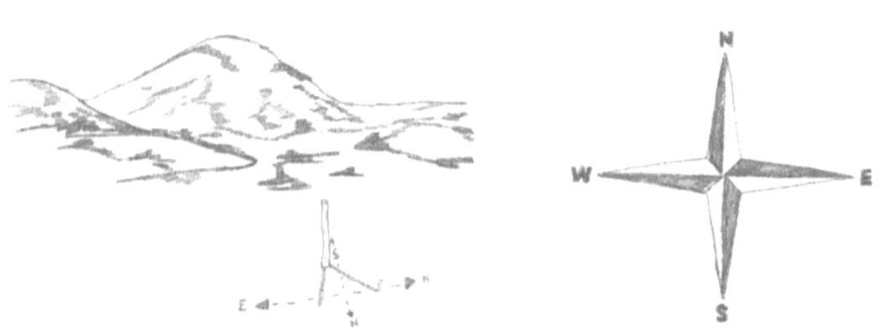

Figure 129. Visual Bearing. This figure illustrates and provides a diagram of a distant visual bearing used to stay in the direction of travel.

Blazing and Breadcrumbing
Primitive Navigation and Self Rescue

When travelling, if a visual bearing or is blocked by terrain, blazing and breadcrumbing can help a person stay in their intended travel direction. Maintaining a line of sight when travelling through a forest, dense bush or terrain that changes elevation can make using a visual bearing to travel almost impossible. Blazing and breadcrumbing can help a person travel in a straight line. Both can also be used to direct rescuers to the location of the person if they are lost. Blazing a trail involves cutting into the bark of a tree to create a visual wound. If the bark is not entirely cut away from the tree, it can cover the visible wound. Blazing can also result in the tree dying and should only be used if it is the only option and should not be sued for training. Breadcrumbing is the best option for real-life situations and training. It involves leaving a trail of stones or sticks. Breadcrumbing is more reliable and does not damage the environment. Breadcrumbs can be lined up to keep a straight line of travel. The technique can be easily seen and allow rescuers to follow a person that is attempting a self-rescue. Breadcrumbing works even when crawling through dense bush or jungle.
Strengths: Breadcrumbing can use almost limitless resources to create a path people can follow.
Weakness: Blazing can kill trees and can be challenging to line up when travelling.
Materials: Trees for blazing and rocks, sticks, any physical object that can be aligned to keep a straight line of travel.

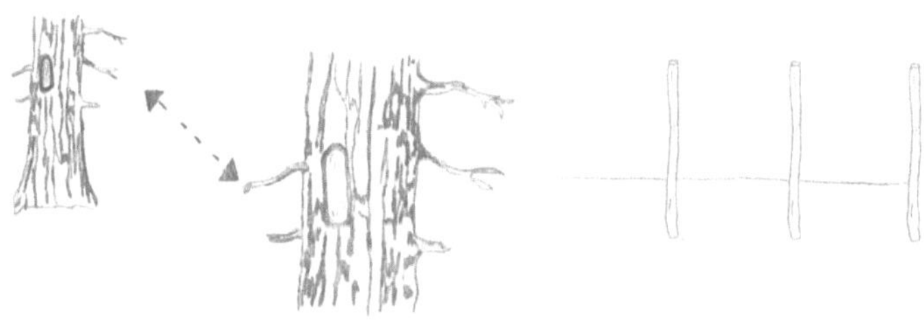

Figure 130. Blazing and Breadcrumbing. This figure illustrates and provides a diagram of blazing and breadcrumbing.

Streams and Rivers
Primitive Navigation and Self Rescue

Streams and rivers can be a more suitable method of travel and faster than bushwacking through dense underbrush. It is necessary to evaluate the conditions before deciding to use a river or stream as a mode of travel. Conditions will vary and change due to the time of year and terrain. Rafts can be constructed and used to navigate a river, depending on the flow rate and hazards. Dry streams and river beds can also provide a more comfortable and faster path to traverse than dense jungle and underbrush. Dry river beds can be dangerous if the area is prone to flash flooding. Dry rivers and streams with high canyon walls are especially prone to flash floods and limit escape avenues. Since many people live along streams and rivers, they can be an excellent travel method to reach civilization provided they meet specific safety criteria. All rivers will flow from north to south in the northern hemisphere and south to north in the southern hemisphere. They may twist and turn, so identifying one direction is impossible based on rivers water flow. Rivers and streams can be a great location to try to signal for rescue.

Strengths: Rivers and streams can provide a more efficient travel mode and increase the chance of receiving rescue.

Weakness: Flooded rivers, rapids, high canyon walls and flash floods may increase the risk of injury or death.

Materials: Rafts and primitive floatation devices can increase efficiency when travelling.

Figure 131. Streams and Rivers. This figure illustrates and provides a diagram of rivers and streams.

Reference:

101knots.com. (2021, January 31st). Figure 8 Knot. Retrieved from
https://www.101knots.com: https://www.101knots.com/figure-8-knot.html

Boutenko, S. (2013). Wild Edibles. Berkeley: North Atlantic Books.

BoyScoutsofAmerica. (2021, January 29th). How to Tie a Square Knot. Retrieved from
https://scoutlife.org/:
https://scoutlife.org/outdoors/outdoorarticles/147528/how-to-tie-a-square-knot

Cheeke, P., Piacente, S., & Oleszek, W. (2019, October 6th). Anti-inflammatory and anti-
arthritic effects of yucca schidigera: A review. Retrieved from
https://www.ncbi.nlm.nih.gov:
https://www.ncbi.nlm.nih.gov/pmc/articles/PMC1440857/

Drugs.com. (2018, November 29th). Prickly Pear. Retrieved from Drugs.com:
https://www.drugs.com/npp/prickly-pear.html

Edible Wild Food. (2019, September 12th). Henbit Lamium amplexicaule. Retrieved from
https://www.ediblewildfood.com/henbit.aspx#:~:text=Henbit%20can%20be%2
0consumed%20fresh,in%20iron%2C%20vitamins%20and%20fibre.

en.wikipedia.org. (2021, February 9th). Arapuca. Retrieved from
https://en.wikipedia.org/wiki/Arapuca: https://en.wikipedia.org/wiki/Arapuca

Finke, M.D. 2002. Complete nutrient composition of commercially raised invertebrates used
as food for insectivores. Zoo Biology, 21(3): 269–285.

Fire Effects Information System (FEIS). (2019, May 15th). Diospyros texana. Retrieved
from www.fs.fed.us:
https://www.fs.fed.us/database/feis/plants/tree/diotex/all.html

Food Central. (2019, October 14th). Mustard greens, raw. Retrieved from
https://fdc.nal.usda.gov/: https://fdc.nal.usda.gov/fdc-app.html#/food-
details/342173/nutrients

Food Central. (2019, October 7th). Nuts, acorns, raw. Retrieved from
https://fdc.nal.usda.gov: https://fdc.nal.usda.gov/fdc-app.html#/food-
details/170157/nutrients

Fruitsinfo.com. (2019, May 14th). Texas-persimmon. Retrieved from www.fruitsinfo.com:
https://www.fruitsinfo.com/texas-persimmon.php

Guil-Guerrero, J. L. (2019, May 28th). Nutritional composition of Plantago species (P-major
L., P-lanceolata, L., and P-media L.). Retrieved from
https://www.researchgate.net:
https://www.researchgate.net/publication/261618820_Nutritional_composition_
of_Plantago_species_P-major_L_P-lanceolata_L_and_P-media_L

Helmenstine, A. M. (2021, January 23rd). Edible Insects You Should Try. Retrieved from
        www.thoughtco.com: https://www.thoughtco.com/edible-insects-4134683#:

Herbal Encyclopedia. (2019, April 18th). Onions. Retrieved from
        www.cloverleaffarmherbs.com: https://www.cloverleaffarmherbs.com/onions/

Homesteadtelegraph. (2021, February 7th). Paiute Deadfall Trap. Retrieved from
        https://homesteadtelegraph.wordpress.com/:
        https://homesteadtelegraph.wordpress.com/2015/05/14/paiute-deadfall-trap.

Kane, C. W. (2017). Wild Edible Plants of Texas. United States: Lincoln Town Press.

Moerman, D. E. (1998). Native American Ethnobotany. Portland: Timber Press.

Natural Medicinal Herbs. (2019, April 18th). Wild Onion. Retrieved from
        naturalmedicinalherbs: http://www.naturalmedicinalherbs.net/herbs/a/allium-
        mutabile=wild-onion.php

Natural Medicinal Herbs. (2019, April 3rd). Black Mulberry. Retrieved from Natural
        Medicinal Herbs: http://www.naturalmedicinalherbs.net/herbs/m/morus-
        nigra=black-mulberry.php

Natural Medicinal Herbs. (2019, January 25th). Cat Greenbrier Smilax glauca. Retrieved
        from Natural Medicinal Herbs:
        http://www.naturalmedicinalherbs.net/herbs/s/smilax-glauca=cat-greenbrier.php

Natural Medicinal Herbs. (2019, June 5th). Pokeweed. Retrieved from
        http://www.naturalmedicinalherbs.net:
        http://www.naturalmedicinalherbs.net/herbs/p/phytolacca-
        americana=pokeweed.php

Natural Medicinal Herbs. (2019, May 30th). Chickasaw Plum. Retrieved from
        http://www.naturalmedicinalherbs.net:
        http://www.naturalmedicinalherbs.net/herbs/p/prunus-angustifolia=chickasaw-
        plum.php

Natural Medicinal Herbs. (2019, May 9th). American Persimmon. Retrieved from
        www.naturalmedicinalherbs.net:
        http://www.naturalmedicinalherbs.net/herbs/d/diospyros-virginiana=american-
        persimmon.php

Naturalnavigator.com. (2021, February 14th). How to Navigate using the Moon. Retrieved
        from https://www.naturalnavigator.com:
        https://www.naturalnavigator.com/find-your-way-using/moon/

Nutrition-and-you.com. (2019, August 7th). Sorrel. Retrieved from https://www.nutrition-
        and-you.com: https://www.nutrition-and-you.com/sorrel.html

Nutritiondata. (2019, June 3rd). Plums, wild (Northern Plains Indians). Retrieved from
        https://nutritiondata.self.com: https://nutritiondata.self.com/facts/ethnic-
        foods/10472/2

Plants For A Future. (2018, December 9th). Daucus carota - L. Retrieved from Plants For A Future: https://pfaf.org/user/Plant.aspx?LatinName=Daucus+carota

Plants For A Future. (2019, April 22nd). Sabal minor - (Jacq.)Pers. Retrieved from Foraging Texas: https://www.foragingtexas.com/2006/12/dwarf-palmetto.html

Plants For A Future. (2019, August 29th). Urtica dioica - L. Retrieved from https://pfaf.org: https://pfaf.org/user/plant.aspx?latinname=Urtica+dioica

Plants For A Future. (2019, February 28th). Chenopodium album - L. Retrieved from Plants For A Future: https://pfaf.org/user/plant.aspx?LatinName=Chenopodium+album

Plants For A Future. (2019, January 1-28-2019). Physalis lanceolata - Michx. Retrieved from Plants For A Future: https://pfaf.org/user/Plant.aspx?LatinName=Physalis+lanceolata

Plants For A Future. (2019, January 3rd). Rubus flagellaris - Willd. Retrieved from Plants For A Future: https://pfaf.org/user/Plant.aspx?LatinName=Rubus+flagellaris

Plants For A Future. (2019, January 5th). Rumex crispus - L. Retrieved from Plants For A Future: https://pfaf.org/user/plant.aspx?LatinName=Rumex+crispus

Plants For A Future. (2019, July 16th). Rosa blanda - Aiton. Retrieved from https://pfaf.org: https://pfaf.org/user/Plant.aspx?LatinName=Rosa+blanda

Plants For A Future. (2019, July 9th). Portulaca oleracea - L. Retrieved from https://pfaf.org/user: https://pfaf.org/user/plant.aspx?LatinName=Portulaca+oleracea

Plants For A Future. (2019, May 1st). Carya illinoinensis - (Wangenh.)K.Koch. Retrieved from https://pfaf.org: https://pfaf.org/user/Plant.aspx?LatinName=Carya+illinoinensis

Plants For A Future. (2019, May 24th). Pinus taeda - L. Retrieved from https://pfaf.org: https://pfaf.org/user/Plant.aspx?LatinName=Pinus+taeda

Plants For A Future. (2019, May 27th). Plantago major - L. Retrieved from https://pfaf.org/: https://pfaf.org/user/plant.aspx?LatinName=Plantago+major

Plants For A Future. (2019, October 14th). Brassica nigra - (L.)W.D.J.Koch. Retrieved from https://pfaf.org: https://pfaf.org/user/Plant.aspx?LatinName=Brassica+nigra

Plants For A Future. (2019, October 1st). Sambucus nigra - L. Retrieved from https://pfaf.org: https://pfaf.org/user/plant.aspx?latinname=Sambucus+nigra

Plants For A Future. (2019, October 6th). Oxalis acetosella - L. Retrieved from https://pfaf.org: https://pfaf.org/user/plant.aspx?latinname=Oxalis+acetosella

Plants For A Future. (2019, September 15th). Sonchus oleraceus - L. Retrieved from https://pfaf.org: https://pfaf.org/user/Plant.aspx?LatinName=Sonchus+oleraceus

Plants For A Future. (2019, September 16th). Cirsium vulgare - (Savi.)Ten. Retrieved from https://pfaf.org: https://pfaf.org/user/Plant.aspx?LatinName=Cirsium+vulgare

Plants For A Future. (2019, September 17th). Silybum marianum - (L.)Gaertn. Retrieved from https://pfaf.org: https://pfaf.org/user/Plant.aspx?LatinName=Silybum+marianum

Plants For A Future. (2019, September 6th). Helianthus annuus - L. Retrieved from https://pfaf.org: https://pfaf.org/user/plant.aspx?LatinName=Helianthus+annuus

Plants For A Future. (2020, July 12th). Daucus carota - L.. Retrieved from https://pfaf.org/: https://pfaf.org/user/Plant.aspx?LatinName=Daucus+carota

Prindle, T. (2018, December 7th). CATTAIL. Retrieved from NativeTech: Native American Technology and Art : http://www.nativetech.org/plantgath/cattail.htm

Quaschning, V. (2021, February 13th). The Sun as an Energy Resource. Retrieved from https://www.volker-quaschning.de: https://www.volker-quaschning.de/articles/fundamentals1/index.php

Rumpold, B.A., and O.K. Schlüter. 2013. Nutritional composition and safety aspects of edible insects. Mol. Nutr. Food Res. 57:802–823.

ScienceOnline. (2021, February 13th). Sundials and Latitude. Retrieved from https://www.youtube.com: https://www.youtube.com/watch?v=WXiakqRWcHc

Shetty, A., Rana, M., & Preetham, S. (2019, October 17th). Cactus: a medicinal food. Retrieved from https://www.ncbi.nlm.nih.gov: https://www.ncbi.nlm.nih.gov/pmc/articles/PMC3550841/

Singh, D. J. (2019, Januuary 22nd). 5 Amazing Health Benefits of Muscadine Grapes (Vitis Rotundifolia). Retrieved from Ayur Times: https://www.ayurtimes.com/muscadine-grapes/

Smith, T. (2019, January 9th). Duckweed. Retrieved from Feedipedia: https://www.feedipedia.org/node/15306

Stevens, M. (2018, December 7th). BROAD-LEAVED Cattail . Retrieved from USDA Plant Guide: https://plants.usda.gov/plantguide/pdf/cs_tyla.pdf

Tull, D. (1999). Edible and Useful Plants of Texas and the Southwest. Austin: University of Texas Press.

USDA. (2018, December 8th). Cattail, Narrow Leaf Shoots (Northern Plains Indians). Retrieved from USDA Food Composition Databases: https://ndb.nal.usda.gov/ndb/foods/show/35195?

USDA. (2018, November 18th). BLACK WALNUTS. Retrieved from USDA Food Composition Database: https://ndb.nal.usda.gov/ndb/foods/

USDA. (2018, November 21st). Blackberries . Retrieved from USDA Database: https://ndb.nal.usda.gov/ndb/foods

USDA. (2019, April 19th). Onions, raw . Retrieved from USDA Food Composition Databases : https://ndb.nal.usda.gov/ndb/foods/show/11282?

USDA. (2019, April 22nd). Hearts of palm, raw . Retrieved from USDA Food Composition Databases : https://ndb.nal.usda.gov/ndb/foods/show/43392?

USDA. (2019, April 4th). Mulberries, raw. Retrieved from USDA Food Composition Databases: https://ndb.nal.usda.gov/ndb/foods/show/09190?

USDA. (2019, August 30th). Stinging Nettles, blanched (Northern Plains Indians). Retrieved from USDA Food Composition Databases: https://ndb.nal.usda.gov/ndb/foods/show/35205?

USDA. (2019, January 28th). Groundcherries, (cape-gooseberries or poha), raw. Retrieved from USDA Food Composition Databases: https://ndb.nal.usda.gov/ndb/foods/show/2245

USDA. (2019, January 5th). Dock, raw. Retrieved from USDA Food Composition Databases: https://ndb.nal.usda.gov/ndb/foods/show/11616?

USDA. (2019, July 17th). Rose Hips, wild (Northern Plains Indians). Retrieved from USDA Food Composition Databases: https://ndb.nal.usda.gov/ndb/foods/show/35203?

USDA. (2019, July 9th). Purslane, raw. Retrieved from USDA Food Composition Databases: https://ndb.nal.usda.gov/ndb/foods/show/11427?

USDA. (2019, June 5th). Pokeberry shoots, (poke), raw. Retrieved from USDA Food Composition Databases: https://ndb.nal.usda.gov/ndb/foods/show/11350?

USDA. (2019, May 2nd). Nuts, pecans. Retrieved from USDA Nutrient Database: https://ndb.nal.usda.gov/ndb/foods/show/12142?

USDA. (2019, May 9th). Persimmons, native, raw. Retrieved from USDA Food Composition Databases: https://ndb.nal.usda.gov/ndb/foods/show/09265?

Verma, R. G. (2014). Rubus Fruticosus (blackberry) use as an hebal medicine. Pharmacognosy reviews, 101-4.

Vorderbruggen, M. (2018, November 8th). Greenbriar. Retrieved from https://www.foragingtexas.com: https://www.foragingtexas.com/2008/08/greenbriar.html

Vorderbruggen, M. (2018, October 10th). Amaranth. Retrieved from https://www.foragingtexas.com: https://www.foragingtexas.com/2008/08/amarath_20.html

Vorderbruggen, M. (2018, October 27th). Dandelion. Retrieved from https://www.foragingtexas.com: https://www.foragingtexas.com/2008/09/dandelion.html

Vorderbruggen, M. (2018, October 27th). Duckweed. Retrieved from
    https://www.foragingtexas.com:
    https://www.foragingtexas.com/2006/08/duckweed.html

Vorderbruggen, M. (2018, October 5th). Queen Anne's Lace/Wild Carrot. Retrieved from
    https://www.foragingtexas.com:
    https://www.foragingtexas.com/2008/08/queen-annes-lace.html

Vorderbruggen, M. (2019, April 21st). Palm - Texas Sabal . Retrieved from Foraging Texas:
    https://www.foragingtexas.com/2005/12/palm-texas-sabal.html

Vorderbruggen, M. (2019, April 2nd). Mulberry. Retrieved from Foraging Texas:
    https://www.foragingtexas.com/2008/08/mulberry.html

Vorderbruggen, M. (2019, August 3rd). Sargassum Seaweed. Retrieved from
    https://www.foragingtexas.com:
    https://www.foragingtexas.com/2011/11/sargassum.html

Vorderbruggen, M. (2019, June 4th). Plum - Wild. Retrieved from
    https://www.foragingtexas.com:
    https://www.foragingtexas.com/2009/07/plum-wild.html

Vorderbruggen, M. (2019, June 4th). Pokeweed/Poke Salat. Retrieved from
    https://www.foragingtexas.com:
    https://www.foragingtexas.com/2006/04/pokeweedpoke-salat.html

Vorderbruggen, M. (2019, May 20th). Loblolly Pine. Retrieved from
    www.foragingtexas.com: https://www.foragingtexas.com/2006/04/loblolly-
    pine.html

Vorderbruggen, M. (2019, November 24th). Henbit. Retrieved from
    https://www.foragingtexas.com:
    https://www.foragingtexas.com/2009/12/henbit.html

Vorderbruggen, M. (2019, October 5th). Wood Sorrel. Retrieved from
    https://www.foragingtexas.com:
    https://www.foragingtexas.com/2008/08/wood-sorel.html

Vorderbruggen, M. (2019, October 7th). Acorn - Oak. Retrieved from
    https://www.foragingtexas.com:
    https://www.foragingtexas.com/2008/08/acorn_20.html

Vorderbruggen, M. (2019, September 13th). Black Walnut. Retrieved from
    https://www.foragingtexas.com:
    https://www.foragingtexas.com/2008/08/black-walnut.html

Vorderbruggen, M. (2019, September 13th). Sow Thistle. Retrieved from
    https://www.foragingtexas.com: https://www.foragingtexas.com/2009/01/sow-
    thistle.html

Vorderbruggen, M. (2019, September 17th). Thistle - Milk. Retrieved from
https://www.foragingtexas.com:
https://www.foragingtexas.com/2006/05/thistle-milk.html

Vorderbruggen, M. (2019, September 5th). Sunflower - Wild. Retrieved from
https://www.foragingtexas.com:
https://www.foragingtexas.com/2009/06/sunflower-wild.html

WebMD. (2018, December 24th). DANDELION. Retrieved from WebMD:
https://www.webmd.com/vitamins/ai/ingredientmono-706/dandelion

WebMD. (2018, November 14th). Bamboo. Retrieved from WebMD:
https://www.webmd.com/vitamins/ai/ingredientmono-585/bamboo

WebMD. (2019, April 3rd). White Mulberry. Retrieved from WebMD:
https://www.webmd.com/vitamins/ai/ingredientmono-1250/white-mulberry

WebMD. (2019, January 9th). DUCKWEED. Retrieved from WebMD:
https://www.webmd.com/vitamins/ai/ingredientmono-426/duckweed

Wild Edible Food (2019, February 2nd). Henbit Lamium amplexicaule. Retrieved from
Edible Wild Food: https://www.ediblewildfood.com/henbit.aspx

Yende, S. R., Harle, U. N., & Chaugule, B. B. (2019, August 4th). Therapeutic potential and
health benefits of Sargassum species. Retrieved from
https://www.ncbi.nlm.nih.gov:
https://www.ncbi.nlm.nih.gov/pmc/articles/PMC3931196/

Yetman, D. (2012). 50 Common Edible & Useful Plants of the Southwest. Tucson: Arizona.

ABOUT THE AUTHOR

Dr Wes Adams is a Professor of Kinesiology and Education. He has taught at both the community college and university level. Dr Adams currently has 20 years of full-time teaching experience in higher education. Following the advice of Master Yoda, "Pass on what you have learned", he started writing books on subjects he teaches (Master Yoda, Star Wars: The Empire Strikes Back, 1980). He believes that it is essential to share his experience with students and new instructors entering the field. Dr Adams takes a project-based approach to ensure students reach the upper levels of learning (e.g., Bloom's Taxonomy). His research focuses on how to use technology to influence education.

www.ingramcontent.com/pod-product-compliance
Lightning Source LLC
Chambersburg PA
CBHW031313250726
48656CB00005B/1771

Secretary of Defense within seven years of relief from active duty as a regular commissioned officer of the Armed Forces.

Proclamation 9570-National Day of Patriotic Devotion.

January 23, 2017

President Donald Trump signed the following:

Memorandum on the Federal Civilian Employee Hiring Freeze.

Presidential Memorandum Regarding the Mexico City Policy (bans U.S. aid from supporting organizations that perform or endorse abortions. The "Protecting Life in Global Health Assistance Initiative" broadens the policy).

Presidential Memorandum Regarding Withdrawal of the United States from the Trans-Pacific Partnership Negotiations and Agreement.

January 24, 2017

Toyota Motor Corp to add 400 jobs and invest $600 million in an Indiana plant.

Keystone XL and Dakota Access pipelines to continue construction, creating an estimated 42,000 jobs and $2 billion in economic benefits.

President Donald Trump signed the following:

Executive Order EO 13766-Expediting Environmental Reviews and Approvals for High Priority Infrastructure Projects.

Presidential Memorandum Regarding Construction of American Pipelines.

Presidential Memorandum Regarding Construction of the Keystone XL Pipeline.

Presidential Memorandum Regarding Construction of the Dakota Access Pipeline.

Presidential Memorandum Reducing Regulatory Burdens for Domestic Manufacturing.

January 25, 2017

Stock gains topped $2 trillion in wealth since President Trump was elected.

President Donald Trump signed the following:

Executive Order EO 13767-Border Security and Immigration Enforcement Improvements.

Executive Order EO 13768-Enhancing Public Safety in the Interior of the United States.

Proclamation 9571-National School Choice Week, 2017.

January 27, 2017

President Donald Trump signed the following:

Executive Order EO 13769-Protecting the Nation From Foreign Terrorist Entry Into the United States.

Memorandum on Rebuilding the United States Armed Forces.

January 28, 2017

President Donald Trump signed the following:

Executive Order EO 13770-Ethics Commitments by Executive Branch Appointees.

Memorandum on Organization of the National Security Council and the Homeland Security Council.

Memorandum on the Plan To Defeat the Islamic State of Iraq and Syria.

January 30, 2017

Over the month, logging and mining added 4,000 jobs, up from the -6,300 monthly average over 2016. Jobs in construction reached 36,000 in January, passing the previous year's 12,100 monthly average.

President Donald Trump signed the following:

Executive Order EO 13771-Reducing Regulation and Controlling Regulatory Costs.

January 31, 2017

The civilian unemployment rate, seasonally adjusted for January 2017, was at 4.8 overall, with Black or African American at 7.8, Latino or Hispanic at 5.9, Asian at 3.8, and White at 4.3. In January 2017, nonfarm payroll increased by 227,000 in the U.S. Most came from retail, construction, financial entities, bar and restaurant, and professional and technical services, followed by health care additions. North Dakota led the lowest unemployment rate with 2.6.

The Supplemental Nutrition Assistance Program (SNAP) was at 42,676,312 persons and 21,111,302 households receiving benefits for January 2017. This cost $5,285,568,000 in benefits.

The unemployment rate in Arkansas set a new low in January at 3.7 percent (previous year 4.1) and Oregon set a new low at 4.2 percent, down from the previous year's 5.1 (since 1976).

The DJIA opened the month at 19872.86 and closed the month at 19864.09.

Total illegal alien apprehensions for January 2017: 32,109.

President Donald Trump signed the following:

Approved H.R. 72 / Public Law No. 115–3 GAO Access and Oversight Act of 2017

<u>Notes:</u>

February 2017

February 1, 2017

President Donald Trump signed the following:

Proclamation 9572-National African American History Month, 2017.

February 2, 2017

President Donald Trump signed the following:

Proclamation 9573-American Heart Month, 2017.

February 3, 2017

President Donald Trump signed the following:

Executive Order EO 13772-Core Principles for Regulating the United States Financial System.

Presidential Memorandum on Fiduciary Duty Rule.

February 9, 2017

Intel announced it would invest $7 billion to build a factory in Arizona, creating about 3,000 jobs.

President Donald Trump signed the following:

Executive Order EO 13773-Enforcing Federal Law With Respect to Transnational Criminal Organizations and Preventing International Trafficking.

Executive Order EO 13774-Preventing Violence Against Federal, State, Tribal, and Local Law Enforcement Officers.

Executive Order EO 13775-Providing an Order of Succession Within the Department of Justice.

Executive Order EO 13776-Task Force on Crime Reduction and Public Safety.

February 14, 2017

President Donald Trump signed the following:

Approved H.J. Res. 41 / Public Law No. 115–4 Providing for congressional disapproval under chapter 8 of title 5, United States Code, of a rule submitted by the Securities and Exchange Commission relating to "Disclosure of Payments by Resource Extraction Issuers."

February 16, 2017

President Donald Trump signed the following:

Approved H.J. Res. 38 / Public Law No. 115–5 Disapproving the rule submitted by the Department of the Interior known as the Stream Protection Rule.

February 24, 2017

President Donald Trump signed the following:

Executive Order EO 13777-Enforcing the Regulatory Reform Agenda.

February 26, 2017

U.S. Hasbro Inc. announced manufacturing Play-Doh once again in the U.S. in its Massachusetts factory by the end of 2018.

February 28, 2017

The civilian unemployment rate, seasonally adjusted for February 2017, was at 4.7 overall, with Black or African American at 8.1, Latino or Hispanic at 5.6, Asian at 3.5, and White at 4.1. In February 2017, nonfarm payroll increased by 235,000 in the U.S. Fifty-eight thousand came from construction and another 28,000 from manufacturing. Other job gains came in professional, business, and private education services, healthcare, and mining. American employment soared by 447,000 to over 150 million.

SNAP was at 42,288,650 persons and 20,934,287 households receiving benefits for February 2017. This cost $5,282,011,696 in benefits.

The DJIA opened the month at 19923.81 and closed the month at 20812.24.

Total illegal alien apprehensions for February 2017: 19,330.

President Donald Trump signed the following:

Executive Order EO 13778-Restoring the Rule of Law, Federalism, and Economic Growth by Reviewing the "Waters of the United States" Rule.

Executive Order EO 13779-White House Initiative To Promote Excellence and Innovation at Historically Black Colleges and Universities.

Approved H.R. 255 / Public Law No. 115–6 Promoting Women in Entrepreneurship Act.

Approved H.R. 321 / Public Law No. 115–7 Inspiring the Next Space Pioneers, Innovators, Researchers, and Explorers (INSPIRE) Women Act.

Approved H.J. Res. 40 / Public Law No. 115–8 Providing for congressional disapproval under chapter 8 of title 5, United States Code, of the rule submitted by the Social Security Administration relating to Implementation of the NICS Improvement Amendments Act of 2007.

<u>Notes:</u>

March 2017

March 1, 2017

President Donald Trump signed the following:

Proclamation 9574-American Red Cross Month, 2017.

Proclamation 9575-Irish-American Heritage Month, 2017.

Proclamation 9576-Women's History Month, 2017.

March 3, 2017

AT&T brings 3,000 outsourced jobs back to the U.S.

March 6, 2017

President Donald Trump signed the following:

Executive Order EO 13780-Protecting the Nation From Foreign Terrorist Entry Into the United States.

Memorandum: Implementing Immediate Heightened Screening and Vetting of Applications for Visas and Other Immigration Benefits.

Proclamation 9577-National Consumer Protection Week, 2017.

March 10, 2017

Neil McGill Gorsuch added to the Supreme Court of the United States as an Associate Justice.

March 13, 2017

President Donald Trump signed the following:

Executive Order EO 13781-Comprehensive Plan for Reorganizing the Executive Branch.

Approved H.R. 609 / Public Law No. 115–9 To designate the Department of Veterans Affairs health care center in Center Township, Butler County, Pennsylvania, as the "Abie Abraham VA Clinic."

March 16, 2017

Coal mining returned to Kentucky after President Trump overturns a bill that shuttered the industry, forcing 460 workers to be laid-off in 2012 in the Perry County mine alone.

President Donald Trump signed the following:

Presidential Memorandum Appropriations request for Fiscal Year (FY) 2017.

March 17, 2017

President Donald Trump signed the following:

Proclamation 9578-National Poison Prevention Week, 2017.

March 19, 2017

President Donald Trump signed the following:

Memorandum on Delegation of Authority Under the National Defense Authorization Act for Fiscal Year 2017.

March 20, 2017

President Donald Trump signed the following:

Presidential Memorandum on the Delegation of Authority Under the National Defense Authorization Act for Fiscal Year 2017.

March 21, 2017

President Donald Trump signed the following:

Approved S. 442 / Public Law No. 115–10 National Aeronautics and Space Administration Transition Authorization Act of 2017.

Proclamation 9579-National Agriculture Day, 2017.

March 22, 2017

President Donald Trump signed the following:

Notice–Continuation of the National Emergency With Respect to South Sudan.

Statement on the Observance of Nowruz.

March 24, 2017

Charter Communications committed to invest $25 billion in the U.S. and to hire 20,000 American workers over the next four years. Charter will also invest $17 million to open a new Spanish-language call center in McAllen, Texas, and hire more than 600 workers.

President Donald Trump signed the following:

Proclamation 9580-Greek Independence Day: A National Day of Celebration of Greek and American Democracy, 2017.

March 27, 2017

President Donald Trump signed the following:

Executive Order EO 13782-Revocation of Federal Contracting Executive Orders.

Approved H.J. Res. 37 / Public Law No. 115–11 Disapproving the rule submitted by the Department of Defense, the General Services Administration, and the National Aeronautics and Space Administration relating to the Federal Acquisition Regulation.

Approved H.J. Res. 44 / Public Law No. 115–12 Disapproving the rule submitted by the Department of the Interior relating to Bureau of Land Management regulations that establish the procedures used to prepare, revise, or amend land use plans pursuant to the Federal Land Policy and Management Act of 1976.

Approved H.J. Res. 57 / Public Law No. 115–13 Providing for congressional disapproval under chapter 8 of title 5, United States Code, of the rule submitted by the Department of

Education relating to accountability and State plans under the Elementary and Secondary Education Act of 1965.

Approved H.J. Res. 58 / Public Law No. 115–14 Providing for congressional disapproval under chapter 8 of title 5, United States Code, of the rule submitted by the Department of Education relating to teacher preparation issues.

Presidential Memorandum on The White House Office of American Innovation.

March 28, 2017

President Donald Trump signed the following:

Executive Order EO 13783-Promoting Energy Independence and Economic Growth.

Approved S. 305 / Public Law No. 115–15 Vietnam War Veterans Recognition Act of 2017.

March 29, 2017

President Donald Trump signed the following:

Executive Order EO 13784-Establishing the President's Commission on Combating Drug Addiction and the Opioid Crisis.

Notice–Continuation of the National Emergency With Respect to Significant Malicious Cyber-Enabled Activities.

March 31, 2017

The civilian unemployment rate, seasonally adjusted for March 2017, was at 4.5 overall, with Black or African American at 8.0, Latino or Hispanic at 5.1, Asian at 3.3, and White at 3.9. In March 2017, nonfarm payroll increased by 98,000 in the U.S. The civilian labor force grew by 145,000. Professional and business services had the greatest gains, while mining followed, adding 11,000 jobs.

Unemployment finished lower in March 2017 than 2016 in 336 of 388 metropolitan areas. Leading these states were the cities of Ocean City, New Jersey (−2.8 percentage points) and Grand Junction, Colorado (−2.7 points), with seventy-four others reporting declines of at least a 1.0 percentage point.

SNAP was at 42,204,555 persons and 20,923,034 households receiving benefits for March 2017. This cost $5,259,670,250 in benefits.

The DJIA opened the month at 20957.29 and closed the month at 20663.22.

Total illegal alien apprehensions for March 2017: 12,750.

In March, 93.3 percent of the Manufacturers' Outlook Survey from the National Association of Manufacturers (NAM) respondents was positive about their company's outlook. This was an all-time high in the 20-year history of the survey. (See Note on this in the September 30 entry.)

President Donald Trump signed the following:

Executive Order EO 13785-Establishing Enhanced Collection and Enforcement of Antidumping and Countervailing Duties and Violations of Trade and Customs Laws.

Executive Order EO 13786-Omnibus Report on Significant Trade Deficits.

Executive Order EO 13787-Providing an Order of Succession Within the Department of Justice.

Approved H.R. 1362 / Public Law No. 115–16 To name the Department of Veterans Affairs community-based outpatient clinic in Pago Pago, American Samoa, the Faleomavaega Eni Fa'aua'a Hunkin VA Clinic.

Approved H.J. Res. 42 / Public Law No.115-17 Disapproving the rule submitted by the Department of Labor relating to drug testing of unemployment compensation applicants.

Approved S.J. Res. 1 / Public Law No. 115–18 Approving the location of a memorial to commemorate and honor the members of the Armed Forces who served on active duty in support of Operation Desert Storm or Operation Desert Shield.

Proclamation 9581-Cancer Control Month, 2017.

Proclamation 9582-National Child Abuse Prevention Month, 2017.

Proclamation 9583-National Donate Life Month, 2017.

Proclamation 9584-National Financial Capability Month, 2017.

Proclamation 9585-National Sexual Assault Awareness and Prevention Month, 2017.

Proclamation 9586-World Autism Awareness Day, 2017.

<u>Notes:</u>

April 2017

April 3, 2017

President Donald Trump signed the following:

Approved H.R. 1228 / Public Law No. 115–19 To provide for the appointment of members of the Board of Directors of the Office of Compliance to replace members whose terms expire during 2017, and for other purposes.

Approved H.J. Res. 69 / Public Law No. 115–20 Providing for congressional disapproval under chapter 8 of title 5, United States Code, of the final rule of the Department of the Interior relating to "Non-Subsistence Take of Wildlife, and Public Participation and Closure Procedures, on National Wildlife Refuges in Alaska."

Approved H.J. Res. 83 / Public Law No. 115–21 Disapproving the rule submitted by the Department of Labor relating to "Clarification of Employer's Continuing Obligation to Make and Maintain an Accurate Record of Each Recordable Injury and Illness."

Approved S.J. Res. 34 / Public Law No. 115–22 Providing for congressional disapproval under chapter 8 of title 5, United States Code, of the rule submitted by the Federal Communications Commission relating to "Protecting the Privacy of Customers of Broadband and Other Telecommunications Services."

Presidential Memorandum on the Principles for Reforming the Military Selective Service Process.

Proclamation 9587-National Crime Victims' Rights Week, 2017.

April 4, 2017

Peabody Energy Corp, the U.S.'s largest coal miner, returned after bankruptcy and plant closings.

President Donald Trump signed the following:

Memorandum on Organization of the National Security Council, the Homeland Security Council, and Subcommittees.

April 5, 2017

President Donald Trump signed the following:

Proclamation 9588-Honoring the Memory of John Glenn.

April 6, 2017

President Donald Trump signed the following:

Proclamation 9589-Education and Sharing Day, U.S.A., 2017.

Notice–Continuation of the National Emergency With Respect to Somalia.

April 7, 2017

President Donald Trump signed the following:

Proclamation 9590-Pan American Day and Pan American Week, 2017.

Proclamation 9591-National Former Prisoner of War Recognition Day, 2017.

April 8, 2017

President Donald Trump signed the following:

Presidential Memorandum on a Letter from the President to the Speaker of the House of Representatives and the President Pro Tempore of the Senate.

April 11, 2017

President Donald Trump signed the following:

Presidential Memorandum on a Letter from the President to the President of the Senate.

April 12, 2017

President Donald Trump signed the following:

Presidential Memorandum on the Delegation of Authority under the National Defense Authorization Act for Fiscal Year 2017 to the Director of the Federal Bureau.

April 13, 2017

President Donald Trump signed the following:

Approved H.J. Res. 43 / Public Law No. 115–23 Providing for congressional disapproval under chapter 8 of title 5, United States Code, of the final rule submitted by Secretary of Health and Human Services relating to compliance with title X requirements by project recipients in selecting subrecipients.

Approved H.J. Res. 67 / Public Law No. 115–24 Disapproving the rule submitted by the Department of Labor relating to savings arrangements established by qualified State political subdivisions for non-governmental employees.

April 14, 2017

President Donald Trump signed the following:

Proclamation 9592-National Park Week, 2017.

April 18, 2017

President Donald Trump signed the following:

Executive Order EO 13788-Buy American and Hire American.

Approved H.R. 353 / Public Law No. 115–25 Weather Research and Forecasting Innovation Act of 2017.

April 19, 2017

President Donald Trump signed the following:

Approved S. 544 / Public Law No. 115–26 To amend the Veterans Access, Choice, and Accountability Act of 2014 to modify the termination date for the Veterans Choice Program, and for other purposes.

Approved S.J. Res. 30 / Public Law No. 115–27 Providing for the reappointment of Steve Case as a citizen regent of the Board of Regents of the Smithsonian Institution.

Approved S.J. Res. 35 / Public Law No. 115–28 Providing for the appointment of Michael Govan as a citizen regent of the Board of Regents of the Smithsonian Institution.

Approved S.J. Res. 36 / Public Law No. 115–29 Providing for the appointment of Roger W. Ferguson as a citizen regent of the Board of Regents of the Smithsonian Institution.
April 20, 2017.

April 20, 2017

President Donald Trump signed the following:

Presidential Memorandum on Steel Imports and Threats to National Security.

Presidential Memorandum on the Global Magnitsky Human Rights Accountability Act.

April 21, 2017

President Donald Trump signed the following:

Executive Order EO 13789-Identifying and Reducing Tax Regulatory Burdens.

Presidential Memorandum on Orderly Liquidation Authority Review.

Presidential Memorandum on the Financial Stability Oversight Council.

Proclamation 9593-National Volunteer Week, 2017.

April 24, 2017

President Donald Trump signed the following:

Proclamation 9594-Days of Remembrance of Victims of the Holocaust, 2017.

April 25, 2017

President Donald Trump signed the following:

Executive Order EO 13790-Promoting Agriculture and Rural Prosperity in America.

April 26, 2017

President Donald Trump signed the following:

Executive Order EO 13791-Enforcing Statutory Prohibitions on Federal Control of Education.

Executive Order EO 13792-Review of Designations Under the Antiquities Act.

April 27, 2017

President Donald Trump signed the following:

Executive Order EO 13793-Improving Accountability and Whistleblower Protection at the Department of Veterans Affairs.

Presidential Memorandum on the Aluminum Imports and Threats to National Security under the Trade Expansion Act of 1962.

April 28, 2017

President Donald Trump signed the following:

Executive Order EO 13794-Establishment of the American Technology Council.

Executive Order EO 13795-Implementing an America-First Offshore Energy Strategy.

Approved H.J. Res. 99 / Public Law No. 115–30 Making further continuing appropriations for fiscal year 2017, and for other purposes.

Proclamation 9595-Asian American and Pacific Islander Heritage Month, 2017.

Proclamation 9596-Jewish American Heritage Month, 2017.

Proclamation 9597-National Foster Care Month, 2017.

Proclamation 9598-National Physical Fitness and Sports Month, 2017.

Proclamation 9599-Older Americans Month, 2017.

Proclamation 9600-National Charter Schools Week, 2017.

Proclamation 9601-Small Business Week, 2017.

Proclamation 9602-Loyalty Day, 2017.

April 29, 2017

President Donald Trump signed the following:

Executive Order EO 13796-Addressing Trade Agreement Violations and Abuses.

Executive Order EO 13797-Establishment of Office of Trade and Manufacturing Policy.

April 30, 2017

The civilian unemployment rate, seasonally adjusted for April 2017, was at 4.4 overall, with Black or African American at 7.9, Latino or Hispanic at 5.2, Asian at 3.2, and White at 3.9. In April 2017, nonfarm payroll gained 211,000 in the U.S. The employment-to-population ratio grew to 60.2 percent, the highest level since February 2009. Jobs added came in leisure and hospitality (55,000 added), healthcare, social assistance, financial, professional and business services, and mining.

SNAP was at 41,702,765 persons and 20,601,941 households receiving benefits for April 2017. This cost $5,172,794,994 in benefits.

The number of total non-farm job openings rose to 6.0 million in April 2017, the highest on record (since BLS records from 2007). Chicago, Naperville, and Elgin, Illinois saw the largest unemployment rate decrease (−1.7 percentage points), followed by Indianapolis, Carmel, and Anderson, Indiana (−1.6 percentage points).

The DJIA opened the month at 20665.17 and closed the month at 20940.51.

Total illegal alien apprehensions for April 2017: 11,677.

May 2017

May 1, 2017

President Donald Trump signed the following:

Proclamation 9603-National Mental Health Awareness Month, 2017.

Proclamation 9604-Law Day, U.S.A., 2017.

May 4, 2017

President Donald Trump signed the following:

Executive Order 13798-Promoting Free Speech and Religious Liberty.

Proclamation 6905-National Day of Prayer, 2017.

May 5, 2017

President Donald Trump signed the following:

Approved H.R. 244 / Public Law No. 115–31 Consolidated Appropriations Act, 2017.

Proclamation 9606-National Hurricane Preparedness Week, 2017.

Proclamation 9607-Public Service Recognition Week, 2017.

Letter to Congressional Leaders Regarding Designation of Emergency Funding Under the Balanced Budget and Emergency Deficit Control Act of 1985, as Amended.

Letter to Congressional Leaders Designating Funds for Overseas Contingency Operations and the Global War on Terrorism.

May 8, 2017

President Donald Trump signed the following:

Approved H.R. 534 / Public Law No. 115–32 U.S. Wants to Compete for a World Expo Act.

Notice–Continuation of the National Emergency With Respect to Yemen.

May 9, 2017

President Donald Trump signed the following:

Notice–Continuation of the National Emergency With Respect to the Actions of the Government of Syria.

Notice–Continuation of the National Emergency With Respect to the Central African Republic.

Letter to Federal Bureau of Investigation Director James B. Comey, Jr., Informing Him of His Termination and Removal From Office.

May 11, 2017

President Donald Trump signed the following:

Executive Order 13799-Establishment of Presidential Advisory Commission on Election Integrity.

Executive Order 13800-Strengthening the Cybersecurity of Federal Networks and Critical Infrastructure.

May 12, 2017

President Donald Trump signed the following:

Approved S. 496 / Public Law No. 115–33 To repeal the rule issued by the Federal Highway Administration and the Federal Transit Administration entitled "Metropolitan Planning Organization Coordination and Planning Area Reform."

May 13, 2017

President Donald Trump signed the following:

Proclamation 9608-Military Spouse Day, 2017.

Proclamation 9609-Mother's Day, 2017.

Proclamation 9610-National Defense Transportation Day and National Transportation Week, 2017.

May 15, 2017

President Donald Trump signed the following:

Proclamation 9611-Peace Officers Memorial Day and Police Week, 2017.

May 16, 2017

President Donald Trump signed the following:

Approved H.R. 274 / Public Law No. 115–34 Modernizing Government Travel Act.

Notice–Continuation of the National Emergency With Respect to the Stabilization of Iraq.

May 17, 2017

President Donald Trump signed the following:

Approved H.J. Res. 66 / Public Law No. 115–35 Disapproving the rule submitted by the Department of Labor relating to savings arrangements established by States for non-governmental employees.

Presidential Determination on the Sanctions targeting the Iranian Central Bank Pursuant to Section 1245 of the National Defense Authorization Act for Fiscal Year 2012.

Statement on the Appointment of Former Federal Bureau of Investigation Director Robert S. Mueller III as Special Counsel To Oversee the Investigation of Russian Government Efforts To Influence the 2016 Presidential Election and Related Matters.

Presidential Determination Pursuant to Section 1245(d)(4)(B) and (C) of the National Defense Authorization Act for Fiscal Year 2012.

May 19, 2017

President Donald Trump signed the following:

Proclamation 9612-Emergency Medical Services Week, 2017.

Proclamation 9613-National Safe Boating Week, 2017.

Proclamation 9614-World Trade Week, 2017.

Proclamation 9615-Armed Forces Day, 2017.

Proclamation 9616-National Maritime Day, 2017.

May 20, 2017

Saudi King Salman bin Abdulaziz Al Saud signed an agreement for almost $110 billion worth of defense capabilities from the U.S.

May 23, 2017

President Donald Trump signed the following:

Order-Sequestration Order for Fiscal Year 2018 Pursuant to Section 251A of the Balanced Budget and Emergency Deficit Control Act, as Amended.

May 24, 2017

President Donald Trump signed the following:

Proclamation 9617-Prayer for Peace, Memorial Day, 2017.

May 31, 2017

The civilian unemployment rate, seasonally adjusted for May 2017, was at 4.3 overall, with Black or African American at 7.6, Latino or Hispanic at 5.2, Asian at 3.6, and White at 3.7. In May 2017, nonfarm payroll added 138,000 jobs in the U.S. Jobs came primarily in professional and business services, healthcare, bars and restaurants, and mining.

SNAP was at 41,582,510 persons and 20,590,488 households receiving benefits for May 2017. This cost $5,165,871,154 in benefits.

Colorado had the lowest unemployment rate in May (2.3 percent), and six other states reached record/series lows (since 1976), including North Dakota (2.5 percent) Arkansas (3.4 percent), California (4.7 percent), Mississippi (4.9 percent), Oregon (3.6 percent), and Washington (4.5 percent) in May. Also this month, 194 of 388 metropolitan areas reported unemployment rates below the U.S. rate of 4.1 percent. Leaders in this were Bismarck, North Dakota, Fargo, North Dakota-Minnesota, and Ames, Iowa.

The DJIA opened the month at 20962.73 and closed the month at 21008.65.

Total illegal alien apprehensions for May 2017: 15,172.

President Donald Trump signed the following:

Proclamation 9618-African-American Music Appreciation Month, 2017.

Proclamation 9619-Great Outdoors Month, 2017.

Proclamation 9620-National Caribbean-American Heritage Month, 2017.

Proclamation 9621-National Homeownership Month, 2017.

Proclamation 9622-National Ocean Month, 2017.

Memorandum on Suspension of Limitations Under the Jerusalem Embassy Act.

<u>Notes:</u>

June 2017

June 1, 2017

President Trump Announces U.S. Withdrawal From the Paris Climate Accord.

President Donald Trump signed the following:

Presidential Memorandum on Suspension of Limitations under the Jerusalem Embassy Act.

June 2, 2017

President Donald Trump signed the following:

Approved S. 419 / Public Law No. 115–36 Public Safety Officers' Benefits Improvement Act of 2017.

 Approved S. 583 / Public Law No. 115–37 American Law Enforcement Heroes Act of 2017.

June 5, 2017

President Donald Trump signed the following:

Statement on Principles for Reforming the United States Air Traffic Control System.

June 6, 2017

President Donald Trump signed the following:

Approved H.R. 366 / Public Law No. 115–38 DHS Stop Asset and Vehicle Excess Act.

Approved H.R. 375 / Public Law No. 115–39 To designate the Federal building and United States courthouse located at 719 Church Street in Nashville, Tennessee, as the "Fred D. Thompson Federal Building and United States Courthouse."

June 13, 2017

President Donald Trump signed the following:

Notice–Continuation of the National Emergency With Respect to the Actions and Policies of Certain Members of the Government of Belarus and Other Persons To Undermine Democratic Processes or Institutions of Belarus.

Presidential Determination Pursuant to Section 4533(a)(5) of the Defense Production Act of 1950.

June 14, 2017

President Donald Trump signed the following:

Approved H.R. 657 / Public Law No. 115–40 Follow the Rules Act

Proclamation 9623-Flag Day and National Flag Week, 2017.

Memorandum on the Effective Date in Executive Order 13780.

June 15, 2017

President Donald Trump signed the following:

Executive Order 13801-Expanding Apprenticeships in America.

June 16, 2017

President Donald Trump signed the following:

Memorandum on Strengthening the Policy of the United States Toward Cuba.

Proclamation 9624-Father's Day, 2017.

June 19, 2017

President Donald Trump signed the following:

Statement on the Death of Otto F. Warmbier.

Statement on the Observance of Juneteenth.

June 21, 2017

President Donald Trump signed the following:

Executive Order 13802-Amending Executive Order 13597.

Notice–Continuation of the National Emergency With Respect to North Korea.

Notice–Continuation of the National Emergency With Respect to the Western Balkans.

Memorandum on Delegation of Authority Under the Consolidated Appropriations Act, 2017.

June 23, 2017

President Donald Trump signed the following:

Approved S. 1094 / Public Law No. 115–41 Department of Veterans Affairs Accountability and Whistleblower Protection Act of 2017.

June 27, 2017

President Donald Trump signed the following:

Approved S. 1083 / Public Law No. 115–42 To amend section 1214 of title 5, United States Code, to provide for stays during a period that the Merit Systems Protection Board lacks a quorum.

June 29, 2017

President Donald Trump signed the following:

Proclamation 9625-To Modify Duty-Free Treatment Under the Generalized System of Preferences and for Other Purposes.

Memorandum on Delegation of Authority Under the Department of State Authorities Act, Fiscal Year 2017.

Memorandum on Delegation of Authority Under the National Defense Authorization Act for Fiscal Year 1998.

Presidential Memorandum on the Delegation of Authority under the Consolidated Appropriations Act, 2017 to the Secretary of Homeland Security.

June 30, 2017

The civilian unemployment rate, seasonally adjusted for June 2017, was at 4.3 overall, with Black or African American at 7.1, Latino or Hispanic at 4.8, Asian at 3.6, and White at 3.8. In June 2017, nonfarm payroll jumped up 222,000 jobs by the U.S. Jobs were added mostly in business services, healthcare, restaurants, and mining, and manufacturing hit a near three-year high. An increase in women ages 25 to 54 (considered "prime age") in the work force hit 75 percent.

SNAP was at 41,444,641 persons and 20,560,734 households receiving benefits for June 2017. This cost $5,170,806,378 in benefits.

The total non-farm job openings rose to 6.2 million in June, a ten-year high.

The DJIA opened the month at 21030.55 and closed the month at 21349.63.

Total illegal alien apprehensions for June 2017: 16,654.

President Donald Trump signed the following:

Executive Order EO 13803-Reviving the National Space Council.

Approved H.R. 1238 / Public Law No. 115–43 Securing our Agriculture and Food Act.

<u>Notes:</u>

54

July 2017

July 11, 2017

President Donald Trump signed the following:

EO 13804-Allowing Additional Time for Recognizing Positive Actions by the Government of Sudan and Amending Executive Order 13761.

July 14, 2017

President Donald Trump signed the following:

Proclamation 9626-Captive Nations Week, 2017.

July 17, 2017

President Donald Trump signed the following:

Proclamation 9627-Made in America Day and Made in America Week, 2017.

July 18, 2017

U.S. Mining and logging jobs have grown by 42,000 since January 2017.

July 19, 2017

President Donald Trump signed the following:

Executive Order 13805-Establishing a Presidential Advisory Council on Infrastructure.

Notice–Continuation of the National Emergency With Respect to Transnational Criminal Organizations.

July 20, 2017

President Donald Trump signed the following:

Notice–Continuation of the National Emergency With Respect to Transnational Criminal Organizations.

Statement on Health Care Reform Legislation.

July 21, 2017

President Donald Trump signed the following:

Executive Order EO 13806-Assessing and Strengthening the Manufacturing and Defense Industrial Base and Supply Chain Resiliency of the United States.

Memorandum on Continuation of United States Drug Interdiction Assistance to the Government of Colombia.

July 25, 2017

President Donald Trump signed the following:

Statement on Senate Action on Health Care Reform Legislation.

Proclamation 9628-Anniversary of the Americans with Disabilities Act, 2017.

July 26, 2017

Foxconn announces a plan to spend $10 billion over the next three years on a 20,000-square-foot plant in Wisconsin. This will employ up to 13,000 employees, and would the first of several plants in the U.S. heartland.

President Trump, who has never accepted his salary as personal payment, donated his second-quarter presidential salary to the Department of Education. Education Secretary Betsy DeVos stated the funds would go toward hosting a camp for science, technology, engineering and mathematics (STEM) students.

President Donald Trump signed the following:

Proclamation 9629-National Korean War Veterans Armistice Day, 2017.

July 28, 2017

President Donald Trump signed the following:

Statement on North Korea's Intercontinental Ballistic Missile Test.

Notice–Continuation of the National Emergency With Respect to Lebanon.

July 31, 2017

The civilian unemployment rate, seasonally adjusted for July 2017, was at 4.3 overall, with Black or African American at 7.4, Latino or Hispanic at 5.1, Asian at 3.8, and White at 3.7. In July 2017, nonfarm payroll added 222,000 jobs to the U.S economy during a time that unemployment was the lowest since March 2001. This took American employment to a new high of 153.5 million. Bars and restaurants saw the largest increase, with professional and business services and healthcare also rising.

SNAP was at 41,112,143 persons and 20,490,751 households receiving benefits for July 2017. This cost $5,126,492,412 in benefits.

Unemployment rates for July for North Dakota was at 2.2 percent, and Tennessee at 3.4 percent, the lowest ever recorded in those states (BLS statistics since 1976). Employment also jumped in 336 metro areas over the year ending July 2017, with St. George, Utah (up 6.2 percent), Elkhart-Goshen, Indiana (up 5.7 percent), and Sebring, Florida (up 5.4 percent) seeing the best gains.

The DJIA opened the month at 21392.3 and closed the month at 21891.12.

Total illegal alien apprehensions for July 2017: 18,782.

<u>Notes:</u>

August 2017

August 2, 2017

President Donald Trump signed the following:

Approved H.R. 3364 / Public Law No. 115–44 Countering America's Adversaries Through Sanctions Act.

August 4, 2017

Toyota and Mazda announced a joint venture plan to build a $1.6 billion U.S. assembly plant at a to-be-announced location. The plant is expected to manufacture 300,000 vehicles a year and employ 4,000 workers. The plant is planned to open in 2021.

President Donald Trump signed the following:

Approved H.R. 3298 / Public Law No. 115–45 Wounded Officers Recovery Act of 2017.

August 8, 2017

President Donald Trump signed the following:

Presidential Memorandum for the Secretary of Defense.

August 12, 2017

President Donald Trump signed the following:

Approved S. 114 / Public Law No. 115–46 VA Choice and Quality Employment Act of 2017.

August 14, 2017

President Donald Trump signed the following:

Memorandum on Addressing China's Laws, Policies, Practices, and Actions Related to Intellectual Property, Innovation, and Technology.

August 15, 2017

President Donald Trump signed the following:

Executive Order 13807-Establishing Discipline and Accountability in the Environmental Review and Permitting Process for Infrastructure Projects.

Notice–Continuation of the National Emergency With Respect to Export Control Regulations.

August 16, 2017

President Donald Trump signed the following:

Approved H.R. 2210 / Public Law No. 115–47 To designate the community living center of the Department of Veterans Affairs in Butler Township, Butler County, Pennsylvania, as the "Sergeant Joseph George Kusick VA Community Living Center."

Approved H.R. 3218 / Public Law No. 115–48 Harry W. Colmery Veterans Educational Assistance Act of 2017.

August 17, 2017

President Trump begins renegotiating NAFTA with Canada and Mexico for better terms for the U.S.'s interests.

August 18, 2017

President Donald Trump signed the following:

Approved H.R. 374 / Public Law No. 115–49 To remove the sunset provision of section 203 of Public Law 105-384, and for other purposes.

Approved H.R. 510 / Public Law No. 115–50 Rapid DNA Act of 2017.

Approved H.R. 873 / Public Law No. 115–51 Global War on Terrorism War Memorial Act.

Approved H.R. 2430 / Public Law No. 115–52 FDA Reauthorization Act of 2017.

Memorandum on Elevation of the United States Cyber Command to a Unified Combatant Command.

August 20, 2017

President Donald Trump signed the following:

Proclamation 9630-National Employer Support of the Guard and Reserve Week, 2017.
August 22, 2017

President Donald Trump signed the following:

Approved H.R. 339 / Public Law No. 115–53 Northern Mariana Islands Economic Expansion Act.

Approved H.J. Res. 76 / Public Law No. 115–54 Granting the consent and approval of Congress for the Commonwealth of Virginia, the State of Maryland, and the District of Columbia to enter into a compact relating to the establishment of the Washington Metrorail Safety Commission.

August 23, 2017

President Donald Trump signed the following:

Approved H.R. 2288 / Public Law No. 115–55 Veterans Appeals Improvement and Modernization Act of 2017.

August 24, 2017

President Donald Trump signed the following:

Executive Order EO 13808-Imposing Additional Sanctions With Respect to the Situation in Venezuela.

August 25, 2017

President Donald Trump signed the following: Proclamation 9631-Women's Equality Day, 2017.

Memorandum on Military Service by Transgender Individuals.

August 28, 2017

President Donald Trump signed the following:

Executive Order 13809-Restoring State, Tribal, and Local Law Enforcement's Access to Lifesaving Equipment and Resources.

August 30, 2017

President Donald Trump signed the following:

Proclamation 9632-National Preparedness Month, 2017.

August 31, 2017

The civilian unemployment rate, seasonally adjusted for August 2017, was at 4.4 overall, with Black or African American at 7.6, Latino or Hispanic at 5.1, Asian at 3.9, and White at 3.8. In August 2017, nonfarm payroll added 156,000 jobs in the U.S. The largest sectors gaining came in manufacturing, construction, professional and technical services, healthcare, and mining. August is a historically volatile time of the economic year.

SNAP was at 41,052,025 persons and 20,521,794 households receiving benefits for August 2017. This cost $5,172,020,469 in benefits.

Seasonally adjusted unemployment rates for North Dakota (2.3 percent), Idaho (2.9 percent), and Tennessee (3.3 percent) were at record lows. The state unemployment data series began in January 1976. Colorado (2.4 percent), Hawaii (2.6 percent), and New Hampshire (2.7 percent) also had extreme lows for the month.

The DJIA opened the month at 21961.42 and closed the month at 21948.1.

Total illegal alien apprehensions for August 2017: 22,932.

President Donald Trump signed the following:

Proclamation 9633-National Alcohol and Drug Addiction Recovery Month, 2017.

<u>Notes:</u>

September 2017

September 1, 2017

President Donald Trump signed the following:

Proclamation 9634-National Day of Prayer for the Victims of Hurricane Harvey and for Our National Response and Recovery Efforts.

September 7, 2017

Amazon.com announces plans to open a massive second headquarters to expand distribution. Plans include investing $5 billion in construction and hiring 50,000 full-time employees.

September 8, 2017

President Donald Trump signed the following:

Approved H.R. 601 / Public Law No. 115–56 Continuing Appropriations Act, 2018 and Supplemental Appropriations for Disaster Relief Requirements Act, 2017.

Proclamation 9635-National Days of Prayer and Remembrance, 2017.

Proclamation 9636-Patriot Day, 2017.

Memorandum on Delegation of Authority Under the Global Magnitsky Human Rights Accountability Act.

Memorandum on Continuation of the Exercise of Certain Authorities Under the Trading With the Enemy Act.

September 11, 2017

President Donald Trump signed the following:

Notice–Continuation of the National Emergency With Respect to Certain Terrorist Attacks.

September 12, 2017

President Donald Trump signed the following:

Approved H.R. 3732 / Public Law No. 115–57 Emergency Aid to American Survivors of Hurricanes Irma and Jose Overseas Act.

September 13, 2017

President Donald Trump signed the following: Proclamation 9637-National Hispanic Heritage Month, 2017; Proclamation 9637-National POW/MIA Recognition Day, 2017; Order-Regarding the Proposed Acquisition of Lattice Semiconductor Corporation by China Venture Capital Fund Corporation Limited; Presidential Determination on Major Drug Transit or Major Illicit Drug Producing Countries for Fiscal Year 2018.

September 14, 2017

President Donald Trump signed the following:

Approved S.J. Res. 49 / Public Law No. 115–58 Condemning the violence and domestic terrorist attack that took place during events between August 11 and August 12, 2017, in Charlottesville, Virginia, recognizing the first responders who lost their lives while monitoring the events, offering deepest condolences to the families and friends of those individuals who were killed and deepest sympathies and support to those individuals who were injured by the violence, expressing support for the Charlottesville community, rejecting White nationalists, White supremacists, the Ku Klux Klan, neo-Nazis, and other hate groups, and urging the President and the President's Cabinet to use all available resources to address the threats posed by those groups.

September 15, 2017

President Donald Trump signed the following:

Approved H.R. 624 / Public Law No. 115–59 Social Security Number Fraud Prevention Act of 2017.

Approved S. 1616 / Public Law No. 115–60 Bob Dole Congressional Gold Medal Act.

Proclamation 9639-Constitution Day, Citizenship Day, and Constitution Week, 2017.

Proclamation 9640-National Farm Safety and Health Week, 2017.

Proclamation 9641-National Gang Violence Prevention Week, 2017.

Proclamation 9642-National Historically Black Colleges and Universities Week, 2017.

Proclamation 9643-Prescription Opioid and Heroin Epidemic Awareness Week, 2017.

Memorandum on the Thirteenth Quadrennial Review of Military Compensation.

September 18, 2017

President Donald Trump signed the following:

Notice–Continuation of the National Emergency With Respect to Persons Who Commit, Threaten To Commit, or Support Terrorism.

September 21, 2017

President Donald Trump signed the following:

Executive Order 13810-Imposing Additional Sanctions With Respect to North Korea.

September 22, 2017

President Donald Trump signed the following:

Proclamation 9644-Gold Star Mother's and Family's Day, 2017.

September 24, 2017

President Donald Trump signed the following:

Proclamation 9645-Enhancing Vetting Capabilities and Processes for Detecting Attempted Entry Into the United States by Terrorists or Other Public-Safety Threats.

September 25, 2017

President Donald Trump signed the following:

Memorandum on Delegation of Authority Under the Consolidated Appropriations Act, 2017.

Memorandum on Increasing Access to High-Quality Science, Technology, Engineering, and Mathematics (STEM) Education.

September 26, 2017

Private sector companies pledge $300 million to K-12 computer science programs. Companies included Amazon at $50 million, Facebook at $50 million, Google at $50 million, Microsoft at $50 million and Salesforce at $50 million. Lockheed Martin pledged $25 million. Accenture, General Motors and Pluralsight each offered $10 million or more.

September 27, 2017

President Donald Trump signed the following:

Approved H.R. 3110 / Public Law No. 115–61 Financial Stability Oversight Council Insurance Member Continuity Act.

September 28, 2017

President Donald Trump signed the following:
Proclamation 9646-National Disability Employment Awareness Month, 2017.

September 29, 2017

President Donald Trump signed the following:

Executive Order EO 13811-Continuance of Certain Federal Advisory Committees.

Executive Order EO 13812-Revocation of Executive Order Creating Labor-Management Forums.

Approved H.R. 3819 / Public Law No. 115–62 Department of Veterans Affairs Expiring Authorities Act of 2017.

Approved H.R. 3823 / Public Law No. 115–63 Disaster Tax Relief and Airport and Airway Extension Act of 2017.

Approved S. 1866 / Public Law No. 115–64 Hurricanes Harvey, Irma, and Maria Education Relief Act of 2017.

Memorandum on Delegation of Certain Functions and Authorities Under the Countering America's Adversaries Through Sanctions Act of 2017, the Ukraine Freedom Support Act of 2014, and the Support for the Sovereignty, Integrity, Democracy, and Economic Stability of Ukraine Act of 2014.

Proclamation 9647-National Breast Cancer Awareness Month, 2017.

Proclamation 9648-National Cybersecurity Awareness Month, 2017.

Proclamation 9649-National Domestic Violence Awareness Month, 2017.

Proclamation 9650-Child Health Day, 2017.

Presidential Determination on Refugee Admissions for Fiscal Year 2018.

September 30, 2017

The civilian unemployment rate, seasonally adjusted for September 2017, was at 4.2 overall, with Black or African American at 7.0, Latino or Hispanic at 5.1, Asian at 3.6, and White at 3.7. In September 2017, the U.S. was still reeling from the devastation of two hurricanes that ravaged the coastal regions, including Texas, Louisiana, and Florida of the U.S. Hurricane Harvey was the costliest tropical cyclone on record, with damages in excess of a whopping $198 billion. It was followed closely by Hurricane Irma, the fifth costliest at $66 billion. Both reached Category 4 status. A job loss of 33,000 was one result of the storms. Another came in a spike in needed services from new applicants and emergency relief, including massive flood expenses. Jobs loss and layoffs hit bars and restaurants the worst. The storms also nudged up jobs created in other sectors, primarily healthcare, transportation and warehousing, and insurance carriers. Despite the losses and slowdowns, hourly wages ticked up twelve cents to an average of $26.55.

SNAP was at 42,002,501 persons and 20,767,711 households receiving benefits for September 2017. This cost $5,763,699,134 in benefits.

The DJIA opened the month at 21981.77 and closed the month at 22405.09.

Total illegal alien apprehensions for September 2017: 22,906. (This was the end of the fiscal year 2017 and last statistics available at the time of publishing.)

The National Association of Manufacturers' (NAM) Outlook Index outlook survey for the third quarter was released with the following results:

Percentage of Respondents Positive in Their Own Company's Outlook: 89.8% (June: 89.5%)

Small Manufacturers: 85.1% (June: 84.8%)

Medium-Sized Manufacturers: 89.8% (June: 90.6%)

Large Manufacturers: 94.9% (June: 92.8%)

Expected Growth Rate for PRODUCTION Over the Next 12 Months ↑ 4.5% (June: ↑ 4.8%)

Expected Growth Rate for CAPITAL INVESTMENTS Over the Next 12 Months ↑ 2.7% (June: ↑ 3.2%)

Expected Growth Rate for FULL-TIME EMPLOYMENT Over the Next 12 Months ↑ 2.2% (June: ↑ 2.7%)

Expected Growth Rate for EMPLOYEE WAGES Over the Next 12 Months ↑ 2.2% (June: ↑ 2.1%)

NAM Manufacturing Outlook Index 61.0 (June: 60.8 – revised)

Expected Growth Rate for SALES Over the Next 12 Months ↑ 4.5% (June: ↑ 4.8%)

Expected Growth Rate for EXPORTS Over the Next 12 Months ↑ 1.3% (June: ↑ 1.1%)

Expected Growth Rate for PRICES Over the Next 12 Months ↑ 1.8% (June: ↑ 1.7%)

Expected Growth Rate for INVENTORIES Over the Next 12 Months ↑ 1.0% (June: ↑ 1.3%)
Expected Growth Rate for HEALTH INSURANCE COSTS Over the Next 12 Months ↑ 8.3% (June: ↑ 8.4%)

Responses to NAM question: "Do you think the United States is headed in the right direction, or is our country on the wrong track?" RIGHT TRACK: 46.4% WRONG TRACK: 21.4% UNSURE: 32.2% (June: Right Track: 56.9%, Wrong Track: 14.3%, Unsure: 28.9%)

The Manufacturers' Outlook Survey from the National Association of Manufacturers (NAM) saw the highest consecutive three-quarter average at 90.9 percent of respondents having a positive outlook for their company in the survey's history.

The survey also reported that leaders in manufacturing report a significant turnaround in activity over the past 12 months, and are "very upbeat" in their assessment of demand and output going forward. With this improved economic landscape, companies were cautious but optimistic that the policies many yearned for, including pro-growth tax reform, a major infrastructure package, regulatory relief, etc., may now become a reality.

NAM Manufacturing Outlook Index indicated strong levels of confidence in business conditions year-to-date, up from 60.8 in the second quarter to 61.0 in the third quarter. For comparison, the index was at 41.3 a year ago. With the prospects of a revised tax bill, companies reported they would use their increase in capital to expand their businesses (64.3 percent), hire more workers (57.3 percent), increase employee wages and benefits (52.2 percent), and invest more in the community (34.2 percent).

After a manufacturing lull of the workforce, companies reported that finding qualified industrial manufacturing personnel was the biggest issue for the next few years, as well as the need for skilled tool and die, mechanics, electricians, and the need to find young people that will enter and finish apprenticeships were their largest concerns.

Over the next year, 16.7 percent of companies expected an increase in overall sales of more than 10 percent, 33.7 percent an increase of 5 to 10 percent, and 30.3 percent expected an increase of up to 5 percent. Also, 33.7 percent of companies expected production to increase by 5 to 10 percent.

President Donald Trump signed the following:

Presidential Determination With Respect to the Child Soldiers Prevention Act of 2008.

Presidential Determination With Respect to the Efforts of Foreign Governments Regarding Trafficking in Persons.

Notes:

October 2017

October 2, 2017

President Donald Trump signed the following:

Proclamation 9651-Honoring the Victims of the Tragedy in Las Vegas, Nevada.

October 4, 2017

President Donald Trump signed the following:

Memorandum on Integration, Sharing, and Use of National Security Threat Actor Information To Protect Americans.

October 5, 2017

President Donald Trump signed the following:

National Security Presidential Memorandum 7.

Proclamation 9652-German-American Day, 2017

October 6, 2017

President Donald Trump signed the following:

Approved H.R. 2519 / Public Law No. 115–65 The American Legion 100th Anniversary Commemorative Coin Act.

Approved S. 327 / Public Law No. 115–66 Fair Access to Investment Research Act of 2017.

Approved S. 810 / Public Law No. 115–67 To facilitate construction of a bridge on certain property in Christian County, Missouri, and for other purposes.

Approved S. 1141 / Public Law No. 115–68 Women, Peace, and Security Act of 2017.

Proclamation 9655-National Manufacturing Day, 2017.

Proclamation 9653-Fire Prevention Week, 2017.

Proclamation 9654-National School Lunch Week, 2017.

Proclamation 9656-Columbus Day, 2017.

Proclamation 9657-Leif Erikson Day, 2017.

October 8, 2017

President Donald Trump signed the following:

Letter to Congressional Leaders Transmitting a Report on Immigration Principles and Policies.

October 10, 2017

President Donald Trump signed the following:

Proclamation 9658-General Pulaski Memorial Day, 2017.

October 11, 2017

President Donald Trump signed the following:

Memorandum on Delegation of Certain Functions and Authorities Under the Countering America's Adversaries Through Sanctions Act of 2017.

October 12, 2017

President Donald Trump signed the following:

Executive Order EO 13813-Promoting Healthcare Choice and Competition Across the United States.

Presidential Memorandum Regarding the Delegation of Certain Functions and Authorities under the Countering America's Adversaries Through Sanctions Act of 2017 to the Secretary of State, the Secretary of the Treasury, and the Secretary of Homeland Security.

Proclamation 9659-National Energy Awareness Month, 2017.

October 13, 2017

President Donald Trump signed the following:

Proclamation 9660-National Character Counts Week, 2017.

Proclamation 9661-National Forest Products Week, 2017.

Proclamation 9662-Blind Americans Equality Day, 2017.

October 16, 2017

President Donald Trump signed the following:

Notice–Continuation of the National Emergency With Respect to Significant Narcotics Traffickers Centered in Colombia.

October 18, 2017

President Donald Trump signed the following:

Approved H.R. 1117 / Public Law No.115-69 To require the Administrator of the Federal Emergency Management Agency to submit a report regarding certain plans regarding assistance to applicants and grantees during the response to an emergency or disaster.

Approved S. 178 / Public Law No. 115–70 Elder Abuse Prevention and Prosecution Act.

Approved S. 652 / Public Law No. 115–71 Early Hearing Detection and Intervention Act of 2017.

October 19, 2017

Unemployment rate among benefit-eligible recipients declines to 1.3 percent, lowest level since 1973.

October 20, 2017

President Donald Trump signed the following:

Executive Order 13814-Amending Executive Order 13223.

Proclamation 9663-Minority Enterprise Development Week, 2017.

October 23, 2017

President Donald Trump signed the following:

Proclamation 9664-United Nations Day, 2017.

Notice–Continuation of the National Emergency With Respect to the Democratic Republic of the Congo.

October 24, 2017

President Donald Trump signed the following:

Executive Order EO 13815-Resuming the United States Refugee Admissions Program With Enhanced Vetting Capabilities.

October 25, 2017

President Donald Trump signed the following:

Presidential Memorandum for the Secretary of Transportation.

Presidential Memorandum for the Secretary of Transportation Regarding the Unmanned Aircraft Systems Integration Pilot Program.

October 26, 2017

President Donald Trump signed the following:

Approved H.R. 2266 / Public Law No. 115–72 Additional Supplemental Appropriations for Disaster Relief Requirements Act, 2017.

Approved S. 585 / Public Law No. 115–73 Dr. Chris Kirkpatrick Whistleblower Protection Act of 2017.

Presidential Memorandum for the Heads of Executive Departments and Agencies Regarding Combatting the National Drug Demand and Opioid Crisis.

Presidential Memorandum for the Heads of Executive Departments and Agencies Regarding the Temporary Certification for Certain Records Related to the Assassination of President John F. Kennedy.

October 31, 2017

The civilian unemployment rate, seasonally adjusted for October 2017, was at 4.1 overall, with Black or African American at 7.3, Latino or Hispanic at 4.8, Asian at 3.0, and White at 3.5. In October 2017, the U.S. economy began to normalize to pre-hurricane gains, as 261,000 jobs were added. Food and drink-related jobs saw the most growth with 89,000, followed by professional and business services, manufacturing, and healthcare.

SNAP was at 45,641,674 persons and 22,114,761 households receiving benefits for October 2017. This cost $6,625,867,861 in benefits. (This was the end of the fiscal year 2017 and last statistics available at time of publishing.)

Mining and logging lead almost every state with the largest 12-month increase in employment since October 2016, with North Dakota and Texas leading, followed by Vermont and Wyoming. Nevada, Oregon, and Rhode Island led in construction jobs. Hawaii reported the lowest unemployment rate at 2.2 percent, and North Dakota hit 2.5 percent. Alabama (3.6 percent), Hawaii (2.2 percent), and Texas (3.9 percent) set new historic lows.

The DJIA opened the month at 22423.47 and closed the month at 23377.24.

President Donald Trump signed the following:

Proclamation 9665-Critical Infrastructure Security and Resilience Month, 2017.

Proclamation 9666-National Adoption Month, 2017.

Proclamation 9667-National Entrepreneurship Month, 2017.

Proclamation 9668-National Family Caregivers Month, 2017.

Proclamation 9669-National Native American Heritage Month, 2017.

Notice–Continuation of the National Emergency With Respect to Sudan.

<u>Notes:</u>

November 2017

November 1, 2017

President Donald Trump signed the following:

Approved H.J. Res. 111 / Public Law No. 115–74 Providing for congressional disapproval under chapter 8 of title 5, United States Code, of the rule submitted by Bureau of Consumer Financial Protection relating to "Arbitration Agreements."

Proclamation 9670-National Veterans and Military Families Month, 2017.

November 2, 2017

Broadcom Limited, a $100 billion semiconductor company, announced it would officially relocate its home address from Singapore to the U.S., namely Delaware. It also promised to bring $20 billion in annual revenue back. Broadcom employs about 7,500 in the U.S.

President Donald Trump signed the following:

Approved H.R. 1329 / Public Law No. 115–75 Veterans' Compensation Cost-of-Living Adjustment Act of 2017.

Approved H.R. 1616 / Public Law No. 115–76 Strengthening State and Local Cyber Crime Fighting Act of 2017.

Approved H.R. 2989 / Public Law No. 115–77 Frederick Douglass Bicentennial Commission Act.

Approved S. 190 / Public Law No. 115–78 Power and Security Systems (PASS) Act.

Approved S. 504 / Public Law No. 115–79 Asia-Pacific Economic Cooperation Business Travel Cards Act of 2017.

Approved S. 920 / Public Law No. 115–80 National Clinical Care Commission Act.

Approved S. 1617 / Public Law No. 115–81 Javier Vega, Jr. Memorial Act of 2017.

Approved S. 782 / Public Law No. 115–82 Providing Resources, Officers, and Technology To Eradicate Cyber Threats to Our Children Act of 2017.

Statement on House of Representatives Action on Tax Reform Legislation.

Statement on Signing the Frederick Douglass Bicentennial Commission Act.

November 5, 2017

President Donald Trump signed the following:

Statement on the Shooting in Sutherland Springs, Texas.

Proclamation 9671-Honoring the Victims of the Sutherland Springs, Texas, Shooting.

November 6, 2017

President Donald Trump signed the following:

Notice–Continuation of the National Emergency With Respect to Burundi.

Notice–Continuation of the National Emergency With Respect to Iran.

Notice–Continuation of the National Emergency With Respect to the Proliferation of Weapons of Mass Destruction.

November 7, 2017

President Donald Trump signed the following:

Proclamation 9672-Veterans Day, 2017.

November 8, 2017

President Donald Trump signed the following:

Proclamation 9673-World Freedom Day, 2017.

November 9, 2017

Lotte Chemical, Hankook Tire, and other South Korean companies announce plans to build production lines in southern U.S. states. This would be part of a 42-company push to invest $17 billion in the U.S. by 2021. Lotte Chemical will invest $3.1 billion in a petrochemical facility in Louisiana, and Hankook Tire will build a new factory in Clarksville, Tennessee, adding $800 million into the economy. SK Innovation will begin to produce ethylene acryl acid in Texas after acquiring Dow Chemical's EAA business for $370 million.

These companies will add up to 52,000 jobs in the U.S. The Korea Chamber of Commerce and Industry reported that 24 South Korean companies would purchase U.S. products and services worth $57.5 billion, including $22.8 billion in energy sectors, by 2021. Korea also agreed to buy more U.S. military equipment, including the F-35A joint strike fighters, and to upgrade KF-16 fighter jets, as well as Patriot PAC-3 ballistic missiles to address the U.S. trade deficit with South Korea.

November 10, 2017

President Donald Trump signed the following:

Proclamation 9674-Commemoration of the 50th Anniversary of the Vietnam War.

Proclamation 9675-American Education Week, 2017.

Proclamation 9676-National Apprenticeship Week, 2017.

November 15, 2017

President Donald Trump signed the following:

Memorandum on Presidential Determination Pursuant to Section 1245(d)(4)(B) and (C) of the National Defense Authorization Act for Fiscal Year 2012.

November 16, 2017

President Donald Trump signed the following:

Presidential Determination Pursuant to Section 1245(d)(4)(B) and (C) of the National Defense Authorization Act for Fiscal Year 2012.

November 17, 2017

President Donald Trump signed the following:

Approved H.R. 304 / Public Law No. 115–83 Protecting Patient Access to Emergency Medications Act of 2017.

Approved H.R. 3031 / Public Law No. 115–84 TSP Modernization Act of 2017.

Proclamation 9677-National Family Week, 2017.

Proclamation 9678-Thanksgiving Day, 2017.

November 21, 2017

President Donald Trump signed the following:

Approved H.R. 194 / Public Law No. 115–85 Federal Agency Mail Management Act of 2017.

Approved H.R. 1545 / Public Law No. 115–86 VA Prescription Data Accountability Act of 2017.

Approved H.R. 1679 / Public Law No. 115–87 FEMA Accountability, Modernization and Transparency Act of 2017.

Approved H.R. 3243 / Public Law No. 115–88 FITARA Enhancement Act of 2017.

Approved H.R. 3949 / Public Law No. 115–89 Veterans Apprenticeship and Labor Opportunity Reform Act.

Presidential Memorandum for the Director of the Office of Management and Budget Regarding the Delegation of Authority Under the Foreign Aid Transparency and Accountability Act of 2016.

November 28, 2017

The Conference Board Consumer Confidence Index hits a 17-year high of 129.5.

November 30, 2017

The civilian unemployment rate, seasonally adjusted for November 2017, was at 4.1 overall, with Black or African American at 7.2, Latino or Hispanic at 4.8, Asian at 3.0, and White at 3.7. In November 2017, the U.S. added 228,000 jobs, with leaders in the professional and business services, manufacturing, healthcare, and construction/specialty trade contracts. Retail jobs also grew by 18,700 for the upcoming holiday season.

From November 2016 to November 2017, non-farm payroll employment rose in 27 states and Washington, D.C. Utah led with 2.8 percent, followed by Nevada and Texas (both with 2.7 percent). Hawaii reported the lowest unemployment rate of 2.0 percent, followed by North Dakota (2.6 percent), and Nebraska and New Hampshire (both 2.7 percent) for the month.

The DJIA opened the month at 23442.9 and closed the month at 24272.35.

President Trump, who has never accepted his salary as personal payment, donated his third-quarter presidential salary to the Department of Health and Human Services' in efforts to combat the opioid crisis.

President Donald Trump signed the following:

Proclamation 9679-National Impaired Driving Prevention Month, 2017.

Proclamation 9680-World AIDS Day, 2017.

<u>Notes:</u>

December 2017

December 3, 2017

The United States notified the United Nations that it would no longer take part in the Declaration for Refugees and Migrants.

December 4, 2017

President Donald Trump signed the following:

Proclamation 9681-Modifying the Bears Ears National Monument.

Proclamation 9682-Modifying the Grand Staircase-Escalante National Monument.

Memorandum on Delegation of Authority Under Sections 506(a)(2)(A) and 652 of the Foreign Assistance Act of 1961.

December 5, 2017

The Trump administration to wind down the Deferred Action for Childhood Arrivals (DACA) program and as a result, those currently covered would begin losing their protection and work permits on March 6, 2018.

President Donald Trump signed the following:

Presidential Memorandum on Regarding the Delegation of Authority Under Sections 506(a)(2)(A) and 652 of the Foreign Assistance Act of 1961 to the Secretary of State.

December 6, 2017

President Donald Trump signed the following:

Proclamation 9683-Recognizing Jerusalem as the Capital of the State of Israel and Relocating the United States Embassy to Israel to Jerusalem.

Memorandum on Suspension of Limitations under the Jerusalem Embassy Act.

December 7, 2017

President Donald Trump signed the following:

Proclamation 9684-National Pearl Harbor Remembrance Day, 2017.

December 8, 2017

President Donald Trump signed the following:

Executive Order EO 13816-Revising the Seal for the National Credit Union Administration.

Approved H.J. Res. 123 / Public Law No. 115–90 Making further continuing appropriations for fiscal year 2018, and for other purposes.

Proclamation 9685-Human Rights Day, Bill of Rights Day, and Human Rights Week, 2017.

Memorandum on Delaying Submission of the Small Business Administration Report Under the Trade Facilitation and Trade Enforcement Act of 2015.

December 11, 2017

President Donald Trump signed the following:

Presidential Memorandum on Reinvigorating America's Human Space Exploration Program.

December 12, 2017

President Donald Trump signed the following:

Approved H.R. 2810 / Public Law No. 115–91 National Defense Authorization Act for Fiscal Year 2018.

Approved H.R. 4374 / Public Law No. 115–92 To amend the Federal Food, Drug, and Cosmetic Act to authorize additional emergency uses for medical products to reduce deaths and severity of injuries caused by agents of war, and for other purposes.

December 14, 2017

President Trump crosses the all-time record with Senate confirming his twelfth federal appeals court nominee during his first year in office.

President Trump's Administration surpassed the 2:1 ratio on deregulation, eliminating 22 regulations for every new regulation created.

December 18, 2017

President Donald Trump signed the following:

Approved H.R. 228 / Public Law No. 115–93 Indian Employment, Training and Related Services Consolidation Act of 2017.

Approved S. 371 / Public Law No. 115–94 Department of State Authorities Act, Fiscal Year 2017, Improvements Act.

December 20, 2017

President Donald Trump signed the following:

Executive Order EO 13817-A Federal Strategy To Ensure Secure and Reliable Supplies of Critical Minerals.

Executive Order EO 13818-Blocking the Property of Persons Involved in Serious Human Rights Abuse or Corruption.

Approved S. 1266 / Public Law No. 115–95 Enhancing Veteran Care Act.

December 21, 2017

On the battle against ISIS front, under President Trump, ISIS fighters are down to approximately 1,000 (from 3,500 under the previous administration); 15,570 square miles have been liberated from ISIS control (up from 13,200 under the previous administration); approximately 1,930 square miles are still held by ISIS (down from 17,500 under the previous administration); and 5.3 million people have been freed from ISIS (compared to 2.4 under the previous administration).

December 22, 2017

AT&T stated it would pay a $1,000 bonus to over 200,000 US employees after the GOP tax bill was enacted. It also planned to invest an additional $1 billion in the United States in 2018.

As a result of the bill passing, Boeing committed an additional $300 million in investments, including $100 million for corporate giving in charitable areas such as employee gift-matching, education, communities, and veterans and military personnel, $100 million for workforce development in training and education, and $100 million for workplace facilities and infrastructure upgrades for Boeing employees.

Fifth Third Bancorp said it would hike its minimum hourly wage to $15, which would benefit 3,000 hourly employees, and give out a one-time bonus of $1,000 to about 75 percent of its employees.

Wells Fargo also said it would raise its hourly minimum wage to $15, up from $13.50, and planned to donate $400 million to community and nonprofit organizations in 2018.

Comcast NBC Universal stated it would award $1,000 special bonuses to over 100,000 eligible frontline and non-executive employees, contingent upon the repeal of net neutrality. The company also pledged to invest $50 billion within the next five years in infrastructure.

Other bonuses came from Bank of America ($1,000 for employees making up to $150,000 yearly), Sinclair Broadcast Group ($1,000 for about 9,000 employees), and Texas Capital Bank ($1,000 bonus to most employees).

In the weeks following the bill's passage and into 2018, more companies would offer bonuses, higher minimum wages, wage increases, and other employee benefits, including Kansas City Southern, PNC Financial Services, Melaleuca Inc., Aquesta Financial Holdings, First Hawaiian Bank, Bank of Hawaii, AAON, AccuWeather, Aflac, American Airlines, Bank of the Ozarks, BB&T, Citizens Financial Group, Comerica Bank, Copperleaf Assisted Living, Dayton T. Brown Inc., Express Employment Professionals, Fiat Chrysler, JetBlue, National Bank Holdings Corporation, Navient, Southwest Airlines, The Flood Insurance Agency, Turning Point Brands, and Wal-Mart, among others.

The passage of the tax law would also allow companies holding offshore fund to bring overseas cash back into the U.S. for a one-time tax holiday. Companies holding large amounts overseas include GE ($35 billion), Foot Locker ($1 billion), Citrix Systems ($2 billion), Western Digital ($5 billion), Waters Corp. ($3 billion), Ralph Lauren ($1 billion), Microsoft ($128 billion), Oracle ($48 billion), Amgen ($36 billion), Apple ($216 billion), Qualcomm ($30 billion), NetApp ($5 billion), and Cisco Systems ($68 billion).

President Trump issued a statement on his first year in office, covering the new tax bill, the U.S. Gross Domestic Product rise to three percent for two consecutive quarters (the first time in three years), remarking on a seventeen-year low unemployment rate of 4.1 percent, a record 60 new highs in the DJIA, new jobs in manufacturing and mining and logging industries, $5 trillion in wealth added to the U.S. economy, and a seventeen-year high rise to 129.5 in the Conference Board Consumer Confidence Index. His remarks in full can be read here: www.whitehouse.gov/briefings-statements/president-donald-j-trump-year-one-making-america-great/.

President Donald Trump signed the following:

Executive Order EO 13819-Adjustments of Certain Rates of Pay.

Approved H.R. 1370 / Public Law No. 115–96 To amend the Homeland Security Act of 2002 to require the Secretary of Homeland Security to issue Department of Homeland Security-wide guidance and develop training programs as part of the Department of Homeland Security Blue Campaign, and for other purposes.

Approved H.R. 1 / Public Law No. 115–97 To provide for reconciliation pursuant to titles II and V of the concurrent resolution on the budget for fiscal year 2018.

Notes: H.R. 1370 provides fiscal year 2018 appropriations for continuing projects and activities of the Federal Government through Friday, January 19, 2018; continues certain authorizations for the Foreign Intelligence Surveillance Act through Friday, January 19, 2018; provides emergency funding for the Department of Defense related to missile defense and ship repair; extends various public health programs and extends funding for the Children's Health Insurance Program; appropriates funding to the Veterans Choice Fund; and includes a direction regarding the budgetary effects of divisions C and D and certain budget reconciliation Acts; H.R. 1, which provides comprehensive tax reform for individuals and businesses; and repeals the individual mandate under the Affordable Care Act.

December 28, 2017

Dollar General plans to open 900 new brick-and-mortar stores in 2018, and plans to open of a distribution center in Longview, Texas, creating about 400 new jobs.

December 31, 2017

The civilian unemployment rate, seasonally adjusted for December 2017, was at 4.1 overall, with Black or African American at 6.8 (lowest ever), Latino or Hispanic at 4.9, Asian at 2.5, and White at 3.7. In December 2017, the U.S. added 148,000 jobs. The largest increases came in healthcare, construction, manufacturing, bars and restaurants, and professional and business services.

There were 310,531 illegal alien border crossing apprehensions nationwide in 20017 (fiscal year statistic), and the Gross Federal Debt was $20.24 trillion. Of the illegal aliens arrested by ICE, more than 92 percent had criminal convictions or pending criminal charges, were ICE fugitives, or were illegal reentrants.

The DJIA opened the month at 24305.4 and closed the month at 24719.22.

From winning the election on November 8, 2016, the DJIA went from 18251.38 to 24719.22 on the last day of business for 2017. The day President Trump was sworn in on January 20, 2017, the DJIA was 19795.06. This was an increase of nearly 5000 during President Trump's first eleven months in office (the DJIA would continue to steadily climb, closing at 25075.13 on January 4, 2018, for the first time ever, within President Trump's first full year in office).

This sums up President Donald Trump's first year in office, building a solid foundation for his platform of making America great again.

<u>Notes:</u>

<u>Predictions for 2018:</u>